Sigils, Seals and Pentacles

Illustrated Guide to the Occult Design
of Ceremonial Magic

M B JACKSON

GREEN MAGIC

Sigils, Seals and Pentacles © 2024 by Mark Jackson.
All rights reserved. No part of this book may be used or
reproduced in any form without written permission of the
Author, except in the case of quotations in articles and reviews.

Green Magic
Seed Factory
Aller
Langport
Somerset
TA10 0QN
England
www.greenmagicpublishing.com

Designed and typeset by Carrigboy, Wells, UK.
www.carrigboy.co.uk

ISBN 978 1 915580 15 3

GREEN MAGIC

Contents

Sigils, Seals, Pentacles	5
Spirit Sigils	17
Spirit Seals	33
Pentagram and Pentacles	61
Magical Furniture	83
Magical Implements	105
Symbols and Scripts	119
Angelic Spirits	133
Demonic Spirits	167
Further Reading	200

Sigils, Seals, Pentacles

Sigils, seals and pentacles are just some of the graphic devices used in ceremonial magic, an occult practice that revolves around the invocation of angelic, demonic and other spirits for the benefit of the magician. It also involves the use of furniture such as an altar, a table of practice, a circle and triangle of evocation and magical weapons like a wand, cup, sword and dagger to summon, constrain and banish such spirits.

Communicating with spirits involves their invocation or evocation to do the magicians wishes. The two terms are often used interchangeably, although they have different meanings. An invocation is to call in, invite or an appeal to angelic spirits and is part of Theurgy or Angel magic. The evocation or summoning, controlling and commanding of demonic spirits, often at the point of a sword is part of Goetia or Demonic magic. Aleister Crowley defined both terms as 'invoke – call in' and 'evoke – call forth'.

Goetia is the occult practice which the modern mind thinks of as black magic. It is often referred to mistakenly as Necromancy, because of the interchangeability between the terms 'necromancy – communication with the dead' and 'nigromantia – black magic'.

At the centre of each invocation and envocation is the conjuration. A conjuration is the calling up of a spirit using ritual recitation of words or sounds believed to have a magical effect. An incantation summons a thing or action into being with words that are sung, spoken or written. Well known incantaions include Abracadabra, Hocus Pocus, Jingle Jangle, Double, Double, Toil and Trouble.

The terms Calls and Keys are also used interchangeably. A Call is an attempt to communicate with a spirt or spirits. Key is used in the generic sense for any device such as a pentacle or book whose possession entitles the holder to a means of access, as conceived by grimoires such as the Key of Solomon.

These things are a part of a magic tradition that began in the High Medieval period (1050), following the translation of many Greek and Arabic astrological, alchemical and magical texts into Latin. This was expanded from 1200 onwards, when Jewish mysticism from France and Spain began to exert an influence on European Christian occultism.

In the Early Middle Ages (600–1050), magic consisted of medicinal magic and healing with the use of occult substances and formula's, instructions for divination and lists of wonderous properties of gemstones and other natural objects. The influx of new knowledge gave rise to the development of new fields of occult study in natural, astral and ritual magic.

Natural magic enables human beings to know and make use of the occult virtues of natural things, as in the healing properties of plants and crystals and natural phenomena such as magnets and rainbows. Astral magic is the capturing of celestial spirits or rays in engraved stones at astronomically precipitous times. Derived from Greek, Babylonian, Sabian, Egyptian and Neo Platonic magical theory and practice, astral magic requires a profound knowledge of astronomy.

Ritual magic is a form of occult practice that involves the use of rituals, rites and maybe some magical tools. Ceremonial magic is a highly disciplined form of ritual magic, in which ceremony and ritual became the tools used in the magical operation to control with and direct spirits, for the benefit of the magician.

In the Middle Ages, magic became synchronized with Christian dogma and the occult practices of astrology, alchemy and magic were subject to the Christian Church's guidance on such matters. And although these new texts were initially recognized as repositories of valuable new knowledge, by the end of the 13th century they were already being treated as suspicious by the Christian Church.

Image Magic
Talismanic or Image magic was the most common genre of magic translated from Arabic into Latin and consisted of rituals to be

performed over a three-dimensional object (an image or talisman), in order to induce a spirit or heavenly body to imbue it with power.

The magical object could be created by sculpting metal or wax, inscribing a piece of parchment or cloth, or engraving an object like a ring, mirror or knife. Rituals included the invocation of spirits and suffumigations or the ritual burning of incense performed over the image. The combination of rare natural materials, engraved representations and a spiritual source of power was central to image magic. When the rituals were complete, the image was placed somewhere appropriate to the operation, such as on a merchant's stall to increase trade or on the body to protect it from harm.

Image magic depends on occult powers in nature, especially those of celestial origin, many of its sources of power – words, characters, images and spirits – were more controversial and astral magical techniques and practices could be identified with more subversive genres such as necromancy, creating affinities between astral magic and the invocation of demons.

Such was the case with the most complex work of astral magic available to the West, the 'Ghayat al-Hakim – Goal of the Wise', an Arabic compendium drawn from 224 magical sources composed in Spain in the 11th century. This work, better known in the West by its Latin translation of 'Picatrix', introduced itself as a book of necromancy and includes far more dangerous practices, such as animal sacrifices directed to spirits and rituals using human blood, although it does omit certain passages, like the one for creating a divinatory head from a decapitated prisoner.

Judeo-Christian mysticism had a long tradition of invoking both God and his angels for assistance and knowledge. Christianity drew on the beneficent divine power of God, archangels and angels, all other rites drew on the necessary evil force of demons, as was the case with the Jewish tradition of the demonic magic of King Solomon. Magicians by the very performance of their arts, entered into pacts with demons and so became agents of the devil.

In the 13th century, the Italian Dominican priest Thomas Aquinas, described as the most influential thinker of the Middle Ages, viewed Natural Theology or Sacred Doctrine as a science.

He was instrumental in developing a new doctrine that included a belief in witchcraft and demonic magic, a departure from the teachings of his master Albertus Magus.

In his works, he discriminated between licit and illicit forms of image magic, rejecting talismans that included signs, figures or images, *"for they receive their efficacy from an intelligent being to whom the communication is addressed and that being is most likely demonic"*.

At this time, magic was regarded as part of a widespread and dangerously anti-social, demonic cult, leading to the persecution of witches and magicians for practicing black magic. The Christian church first condemned such practices about 800 CE but between 1022 and 1850, it systematically demonized the non-Christian beliefs of Europe.

The result was a charge of heresy for witches, pagans, gnostics, alchemists, magicians, sorcerers and others, leading to the genocide of the Cathars, the Spanish Inquisition, witch burning and magic symbols being associated solely with witchcraft, black magic and devil worship.

But it was not until the publication of the Malleus Maleficorius in Germany by another Dominican priest Heinrich Kramer in 1487, that individuals who practiced things considered witchcraft and sorcery were punished severely.

Written in Latin, the title roughly translates as 'Hammer of the Witches'. It was essentially a guide on how to convict an individual of witchcraft. Kramer made a specific connection between women and Satanic magic that became widespread, using over 100 quotes taken from Thomas Aquinas to do so.

Grimoires

Magicians recorded their magical designs and conjurations in text books called Grimoires, often written in a magical script. Some were more akin to cook books containing 'recipes' for the calling of spirits. Such books are exemplified by those produced during the Renaissance and include Da Occulta Philosophie by Henrich Cornelius Agrippa, the anonymous Aratabel of Magic, the pseudonymous Keys of Solomon and the Heptarchia by Dr. John Dee, among many others.

The Magica Veterum or the Magic of the Ancients is a Latin grimoire of Renaissance ceremonial magic published in 1575 in Switzerland. The title is assumed to be derived from the Hebrew 'Arbota' as the name of the angel the author would have claimed to have learned magic from. The Aratabel mainly focuses on the relationship between humanity, celestial hierarchies and the positive relationship between the two. The Olympian Spirits featured in it are totally original.

Elements of the Aratabel appear in a number of versions of the Sixth and Seventh Books of Moses. Dr. John Dee was influenced by the Aratabel, as Dee did not see his angelic experiments as magical but as religious. Both Dee and the Aratabel begin with prayers to God. As opposed to the Lesser Keys of Solomon which is focused on demonology.

From 1600 onward, with the rise of the Ages of Science, Enlightenment and Reason, the notion of magic faded from the European mind. Occult text books were forgotten and left to gather dust in library archives until rediscovered in the 19th century, when they were given the name 'grimoire' meaning 'magical text book'. Throughout this time, the western occult tradition was carried on by such groups as the Rosicrucian's, Illuminati and Freemasons.

In 1805, Francis Barrett recorded the remaining knowledge of western occultism into one volume titled 'The Magus'. Later in the same century, a revival of ceremonial magic began with the occultist Eliphas Levi. He made a new collection of magical knowledge but, by drawing upon mesmerism, reworked it into a system more compatible with the scientific spirit of the age.

He resurrected an interest in Solomonic magic that has made it the most popular form of ceremonial magic in the modern West. He also integrated divinatory work with the Tarot into a new system, supplying enough information so that any individual could begin to practice ceremonial magic again.

Later in the same century, organizations based on the practice of ceremonial magic began to appear, the most important being the Hermetic Order of the Golden Dawn in England. Golden Dawn member S L Mathers rediscovered many of the older grimoires, including those of Solomonic and Enochian magic, which he mined to include in the Golden Dawn's teachings, publishing several of them.

This effort was followed by that of fellow Golden Dawn member Aleister Crowley, who developed a more psychological orientated magical system based of the Exercise of the Will or Thelema. Crowley and his work were a great influence on the occultism of the late 20th century.

In the 20th century, ceremonial magic spread through the West and although it has never been the most popular practice with occultists, due to its stringent magical requirements, several groups, such as the Ordo Templis Orientalis, have become international organizations. Other influential ceremonial magicians of the 20th century include Dion Fortune, Jack Parsons, Phyllis Seckler, Kenneth Grant, James Lees and Nema Andahadna.

Since the end of the second world war there has been a large market in magical texts including the reprinting of old editions as well as the creation of new grimoires. Published in 1984, the Master Grimoire of Magickal Rites and Ceremonies by Nathan Elkman integrates material from older works into a modernist perspective with little mention of spirits or demons.

After the positive white magic of the 1960s Counter Culture, the 1970s saw a revival of interest in dark magic, including that of Aleister Crowley and Sumerian demonology. This influenced several writers and occultists to develop the fictional work of US horror writer H P Lovecraft, into various spoof or hoax versions of his fictional grimoire of demonic magic called the Necronomicon. Although Lovecraft never produced his own edition, various versions were published and continue to be published. The most famous being the 'Simon' Necronomicon, thought to have been created by American occultist Peter Levenda.

Released in 1977, it is a mixture of re-contextualized Sumerian and Babylonian texts, and the oriental magical system of Aleister Crowley, peppered with references to fictional deities from the Cthuthulhu Mythos created by H P Lovecraft, that feature in his fictional grimoire called 'The Necronomicon', which the 'Simon' claims to be the original of, as do many of the others. Other notable versions include the 'Al Azif – Book of Dead Names', credited to Wilson and Hay, and one attributed to Dr. John Dee.

The history of the Necronomicon is seen to follow a similar path to that of the magic of Solomon, in which a myth or work of fiction has been developed into a recognized form of ceremonial magic.

More recently, a creatively innovative grimoire of demonic magic titled Legion 49 was published in 2014 by Australian artist and occultist Barry William Hale. In this work, Hale employs his version of the Mexican Day of the Dead 'shadow-cut' technique as an alternative to the conventional spirit sigils for Beelzebub and his 49 Servitors. As an addition, he produced the Circle of Beelzebub featuring Beelzebub's sigil and a sigillic recension of the incantation using Austin Osman Spare's 'sigilisation' technique.

In its pre-twentieth century form, ceremonial magic rites were religious actions, and the ritual format partook largely of the nature of religious observances. Although it departed radically from orthodox Christianity, it was not the reverse of Christianity or Judaism as generally supposed, nor did it partake of the perforation of religious rituals. It was in effect, an attempt to derive power from God for the successful control of evil spirits. The God invoked in black magic was not Satan but Yahweh/Jehovah of the Jews and the Holy Trinity of Christianity.

Beginning in the 20th century, contemporary ceremonial magic concerns the disciplines of the self and the art of controlling and directing personal and cosmic powers, which may or may not be personified as demonic or deific forms.

SIGILS, SEALS AND PENTACLES

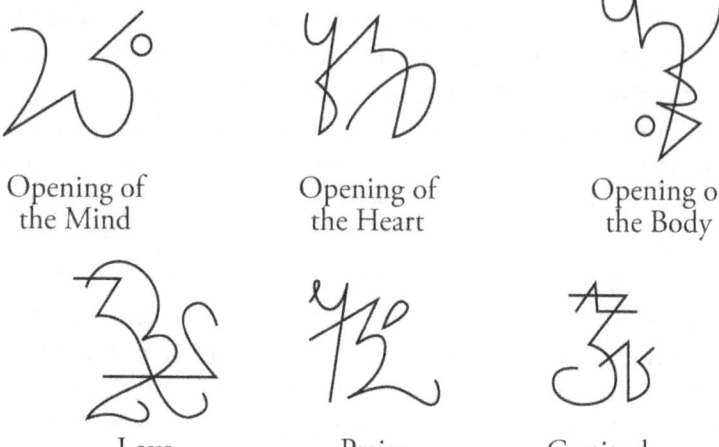

| Opening of the Mind | Opening of the Heart | Opening of the Body |

| Love | Praise | Gratitude |

Healing Sigils - Angel Belvaspata

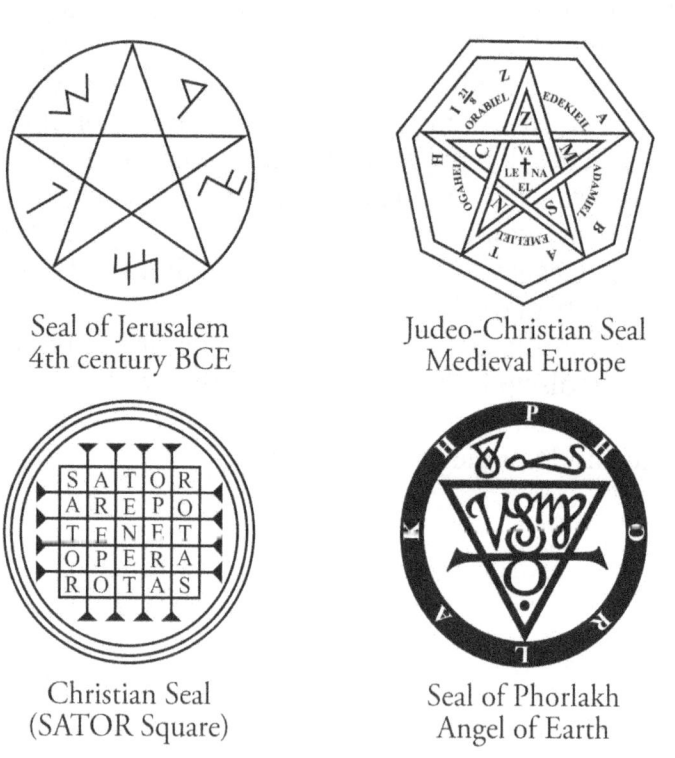

| Seal of Jerusalem 4th century BCE | Judeo-Christian Seal Medieval Europe |

| Christian Seal (SATOR Square) | Seal of Phorlakh Angel of Earth |

Variation in Seal Design

SIGILS, SEALS, PENTACLES

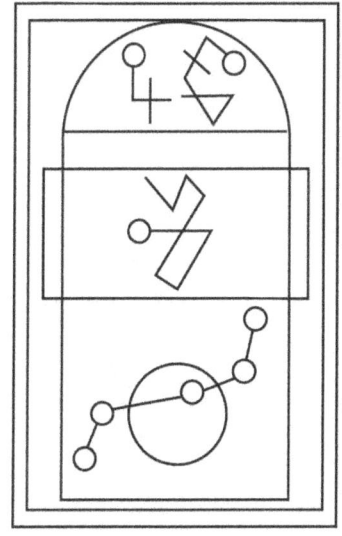
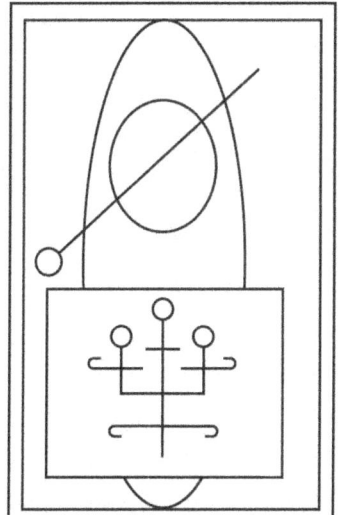

6th Gate - Lord Marduk   7th Gate - Ninib called Adar
Dr. John Dee's Necronomiccon - Philadelphia University (20th c.)

Scorpio   The Serpent Bearer
Seal of the Twelfth Key on   Seal of the Thirteenth Key on
the Twelfth Gate   the Thirteenth Gate

13 Gates of the Necronomiccon - Donald Tyson (21st c.)
Pentacle or Gate Designs of the Necronomicxon

Circle of Solomon used for consecrating Pentacles
(Greater) Key of Solomon

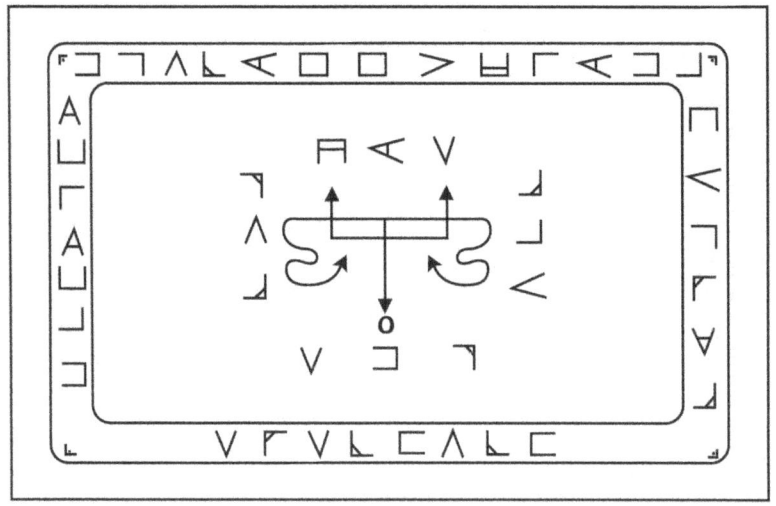

Alter / Table
Al Azif' Necronomicon - Wilson, Turner, Hay, Langford

Examples of Circle and Altar Design

SIGILS, SEALS, PENTACLES

Chaldean (Adamic / Mosaic) - Ashuri / Assyrian Black Letter

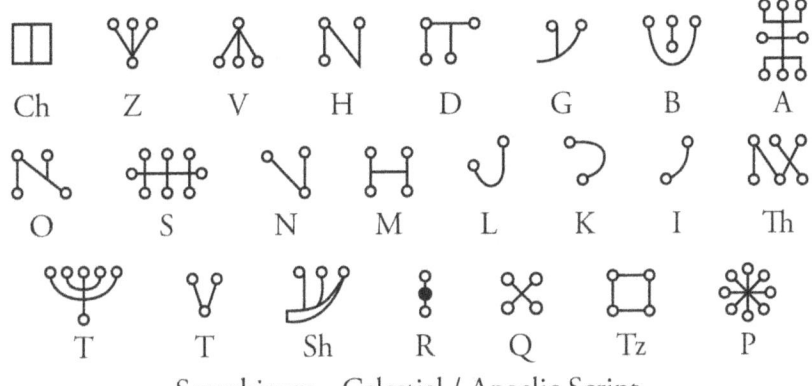

Seraphicum - Celestial / Angelic Script

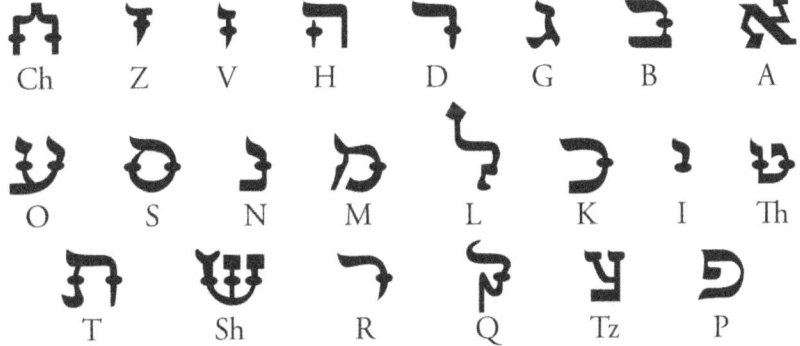

Enochaeum (Torahanic) - Hepburn's Virga Aurea 1616

Magic Script Styles - Chaldean, Celestial / Angelic, Enochian

Spirit Sigils

A spirit sigil is the occult signature of a spirit, being or entity. Sigil is an English term derived from the Latin words sigilla, sigillum and signum, and in terms of magic it is generally understood to mean sign, seal, signature or little picture. Alternatively, sigil may be related to the Hebrew word 'segulah' meaning action, word or something that has a supernatural effect.

As symbols designed for a specific magical purpose, it was from astrology that the word sigil became acknowledged as an occult device with great power. Today, the word sigil has a more general meaning, used to refer to any symbol with magical connotations.

Conventionally, a sigil is a line diagram symbolizing the unpronounceable name of a spirit. Each spirit had its own sigil, a pictorial signature or spiritual autograph representing its 'essence', as to know the name of a spirit gives the magician the ability to command the spirit. In ceremonial magic, the sigil is the representation of the will of the magician and is used to empower the goal of the will through various means.

The concept of a sigil used to represent the name of a spirit became established during the Late Medieval and Renaissance period 1250–1600. Magicians created and studied these symbols, publishing lists of them in magical text books called grimoires. In which they recorded a sigils occult 'alpha-numeric' origins, encoded in magic squares or kamea, their use in the preparation of seals and pentacles and their placement on magical furniture and implements such as the circle, alter, table, wand, sword, dagger and chalice.

By the beginning of the 20th century, science and rationale had played a monumental role in the re-realizing of magic practice. Self-professed adepts likr Aleistair Crowley and Austin Osman Spare, rejected the traditions of ceremonial magic. They took the sigil out of ritual and employed them in their personal quests of mystical exploration as a Monogram of Thought, a graphic symbol created with the sole purpose of fulfilling the magicians desired outcome, a personal desire or set of desires.

Such sigils are formed from the artistic 'binding' of the individual letters of words and statements of desire, they are a major component in the modern practice of Chaos Magick. Witches, Wiccans and Satanists also use sigils to capture 'will' and/or 'intent', condensed into one intricate symbol.

In the early 21st century, Barry William Hale reintroduced Spare's sigilisation technique back into ceremonial magic in his creatively innovative grimoire of demonic magic titled Legion 49. In which, he also replaces the spirit sigil with 'shadow-cuts' derived from the Mexican Day of the Dead tradition.

Sigil Styles

Sigils come in many styles, the most obvious being a spirit signature, the actual name of a spirit written by a spirit, mainly a demon. This often occurs through the process of automatic writing or scrying. Spirits often use obscure alphabets or letter forms and mirror their names or sign them upside down to further disguise them. Often, it's not possible to read them as they are usually a series of separate or connected forms written out in a line, in a way that resembles writing. By contrast, some spirit sigils can be more compact and resemble little pictures.

Over the millennia, planetary spirits have had many different sigils, symbols and characters attached to them, mainly from astrology and alchemy. Others being unique signs created by the magicians for specific rituals.

Modern and post-modern sigils are somewhat revolutionary, whether that be Osman Spare's early 20th century 'sigilisation' technique, the 1970s sigil styles of the various Necronomicon's of that decade or Barry William Hale's innovative 'shadow-cut' sigils of the 21st century.

Spirit Sigils

The classic method for creating a spirit sigil is to use the numerology associated with kamea or magic squares. This stems from the practice of Isosephy, invented by the Greek scholar Pythagoras, circa 600 BCE, in which each letter of the alphabet is assigned to the numbers 1–9. Giving the letters of a word 'a numerical order' which can be traced out on a 3 x 3 magic square.

These spirit sigils are created by converting the name of a spirit to a numerical form using an alpha-numeric code and number square. The location of the numbers within the square are connected in sequence by a line to form an abstract figure that becomes the spirit's sigil or occult signature. The most potent of these sigils are the ones that can be drawn in a single line without taking the pen off the paper.

The style of the sigil is created by drawing an open circle round the first number, then a line is drawn to pass through each number in sequence without the pen leaving the paper and finished with a terminal stroke or closed circle on the last number. The circle and the terminal line denote the beginning and ending of a name or word. A loop is used to denote double letters – EE, and a double bump denotes the use of two letters in the same square – AB. Once devised, the sigil may be mirrored, rotated and perfected.

Rosy Cross Cipher
Various word ciphers are used to create spirit sigils. The Rosy Cross Cipher was created by the Golden Dawn and is based on the Double Star of the Sepher Yetzirah, providing a simpler method of constructing sigils for spirits with Hebrew names. Names in any other language will not work with this cipher.

The Golden Dawn Enochian Rose cipher can be used to create sigils using English. First, draw a circle around the first letter of the entities name. Then draw a connecting line from letter to letter in spelling order until the last letter, when a short terminal stroke is added. The circle and terminal stroke mark the beginning and end of the sigil. If two letters appear on the same line, a loop is added to indicate the letters. A double hump is used if a name has a double letter or two of its letters are represented on the same petal. Other letter ciphers include a version of Agrippa's construction of the 5 x 5 kamea and the QWERTY keyboard letter order.

Aiq Bkr Cipher

This occult cipher for the English alphabet is based on the cabalistic Aiq Bkr cipher for Hebrew. It is the original 'box cipher' for the alphabet and was one of several similar systems described by Agrippa and adapted by the Rosicrucian's and the Freemasons.

As with Hebrew, the English letters of the alphabet are arranged in a 3 x 3 grid. Each square of the grid contains three letters, written across and down, from left to right, the Ampersand is used to equal the number of letters in the Aiq Bkr sequence.

The cipher works by taking the English spelling of the name to be ciphered and locating each letter on the grid. The letter is denoted by its position within the cell and the position of the cell within the grid. When the cipher is written, the script looks like a simple graphic design.

Agrippa also described how the Aiq Bkr characters can be combined to form Olympian Sigils to encode the names of the celestial spirits called the Olympian angels. Although Agrippa showed several such systems, the method shown is based on one provided by Francis Barrett in The Magus.

First, encode the name or word using the Aiq Bkr cipher and condense its form. Next, replace the dots with vertical lines topped by triangles to further encode the sigil. To encode it even further, draw a connecting line joining those letters that stand on the same line in the cipher.

Bind Letters and Symbols

Binding is the ancient technique of graphically combining key letters to form a sigil whose power is derived from the magic art of binding. Bind Runes are the most common form of this technique. Word and Statement sigils also use the binding technique in the arrangement of letters to form sigils. The binding of the individual letters of words and statements is the conceptual basis of Austin Osman Spare's groundbreaking 'sigilization' technique, a cornerstone of the modern art of Chaos Magick.

The signs of the zodiac, the planets and those of the four elements can be bound together to form symbols sometimes referred to as Elemental Sigils. Such sigils were created to represent the names of angels and, with their corresponding symbols and spirits, incorporated into the design of seals, pentacles, amulets and talismans.

Celestial Charakteres
In ancient times, each of the brighter fixed stars possessed its own mythology and image meaning. This occurred especially in Persian magic, renowned for its astrology and astronomy which attached a host of esoteric associations to the stars.

Among Gnostics, Hermetics and Neoplatonists, existed the belief that each star was the heavenly home of a spiritual intelligence – a higher being that might be prevailed upon to intercede with humanity, provided the correct prayers, offerings and devotions were made. When human souls were perfected, they ascended to their rightful place in the heavens to become stars themselves.

The influence of these spiritual creatures made itself felt upon the Earth by means of rays of light that shone down from the stars, transmitting an occult virtue to the places they illuminated. Based on this belief is the astrological concept of aspects or angles between heavenly bodies, each aspect with its own benign or malign influence.

One category of signs developed to represent these heavenly beings are referred to as Celestial Charakteres, quasi-alphabetical signs formed of strokes ending in circles. Also called 'ring letters', they are known to be inspired by the linking of shapes that are to be found in the constellations of the fixed stars of the northern and southern hemispheres.

Such charakteres are an ancient writing which Moses and the prophets used and were forbidden to divulge to the uninitiated. They appear in the Sefer Raziel and other Jewish magical manuscripts attributed to angels, for use in the preparation of amulets. They were also used by the Coptic Church in Late Antiquity 100–500 CE, often for the names of angels.

Magically, they could be used to gain favour, for example, by writing the charakteres or 'hatonet' on the right hand, then wiping them with olive oil and anointing the face with them.

Magical charakteres are not a Jewish invention. The exact origins are not fully known. They came into existence sometime around the 2nd and 3rd century, probably originating from the ancient Greco-Egyptian occult tradition. They do not have a phonetic value, they are purely visual symbols, incomprehensible to humans, used to summon the help of supernatural beings by talking or rather writing to them in their own language, which is why they are referred to as Angelic or Celestial sigils.

Word and Statement Sigils
In the first half of the 20th century, English occultist's including Aleister Crowley and Austin Osman Spare, decided to reform aspects ceremonial magic with a modern-day perspective. Spare developed the technique of 'sigilistation' or the use of sigils and how to empower them outside of ritual.

Spare did not agree with the medieval practice of using sigils, arguing that such supernatural beings were simply complexes in the unconscious and could be actively created through the process of sigilisation, in which the letters of a word or statement of desire or intent, can be reduced to form an appropriate sigil. In a similar manner to that of rune binding.

Spare's unique method of creating and using sigils has had a huge effect on modern occultism. In the 1970s, thanks to another English occultist Kenneth Graham, sigilisation became the cornerstone of Chaos Magick. It has also influenced artists and occultists such as Brion Crysin and Barry William Hale.

SPIRIT SIGILS

Signature of the Demon Leviathan

Signature of the Angel Belvaspata

Spirit Signatures

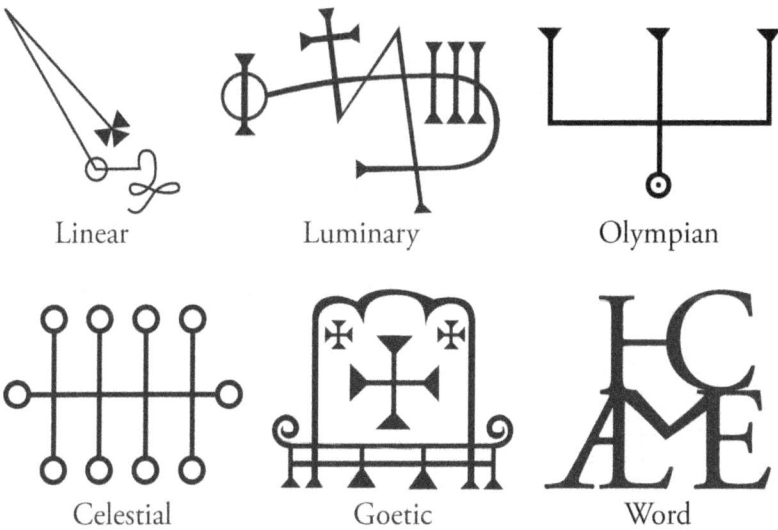

Sigil Styles

SIGILS, SEALS AND PENTACLES

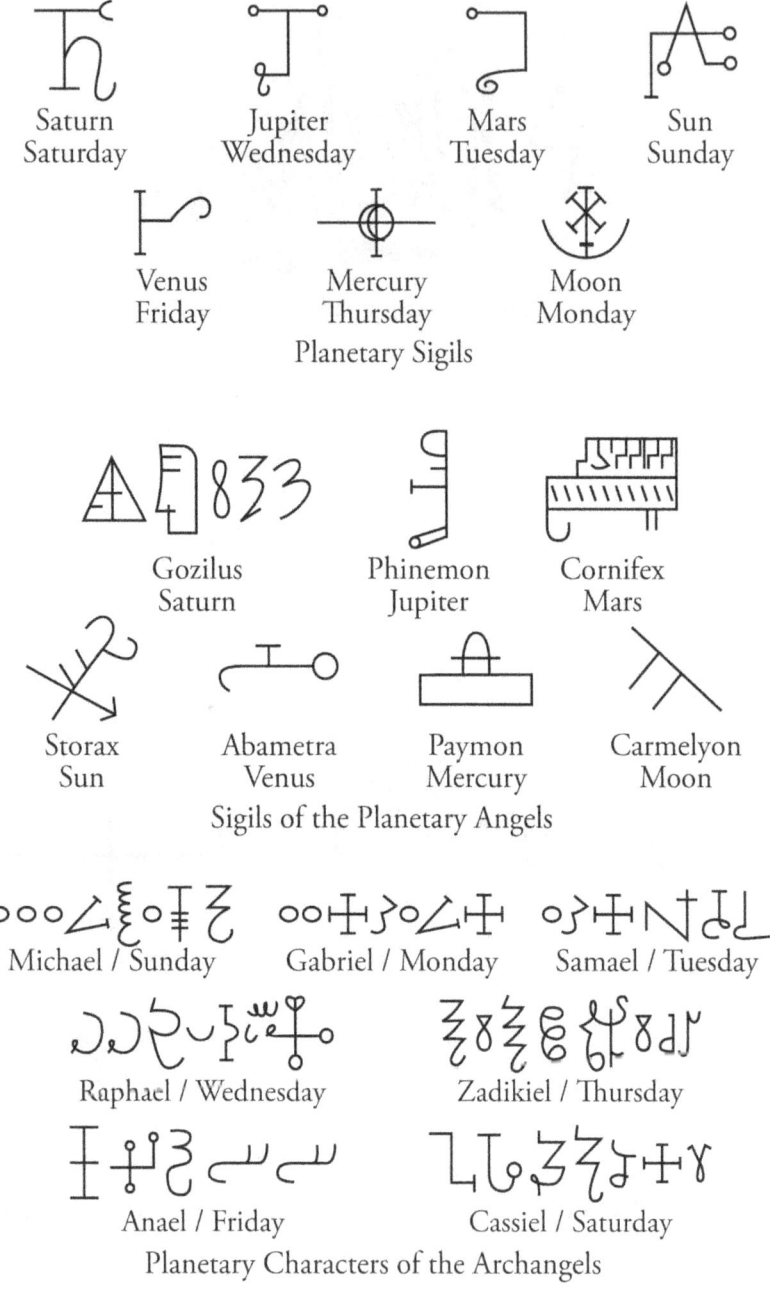

SPIRIT SIGILS

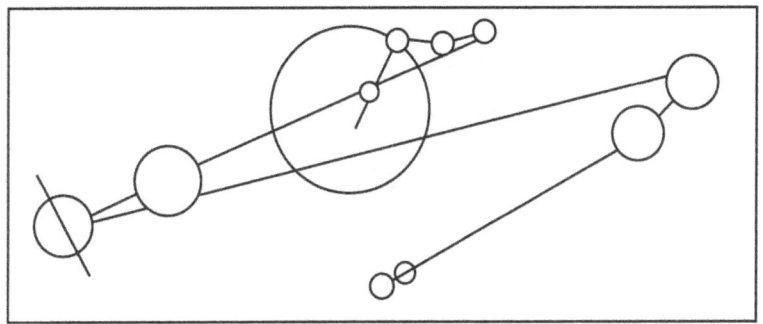

Glyph of Yoggoth
Dr. John Dee's Necronomicon - Philadelphia University Press

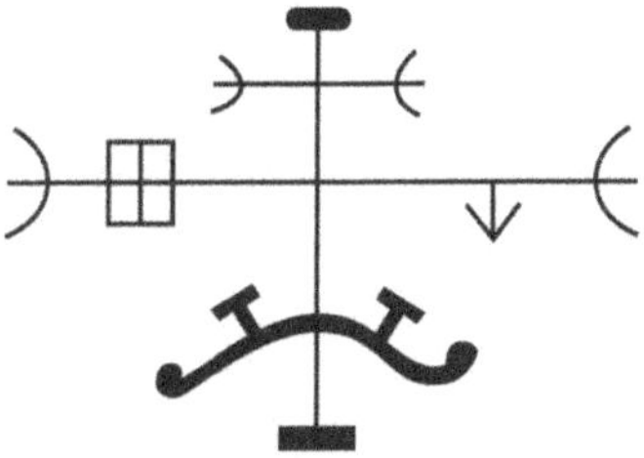

Globes

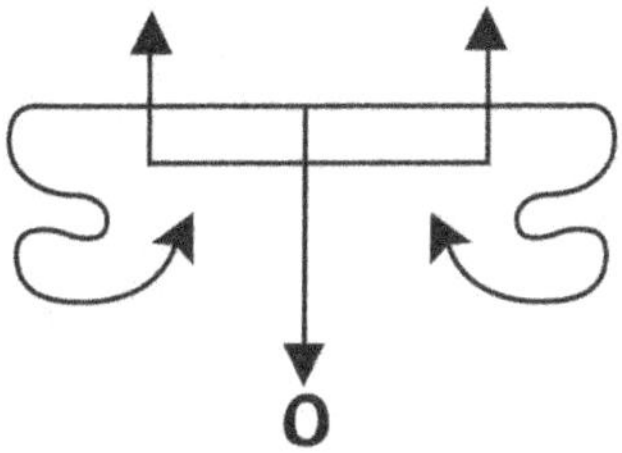

Seal of Yog Sothoth

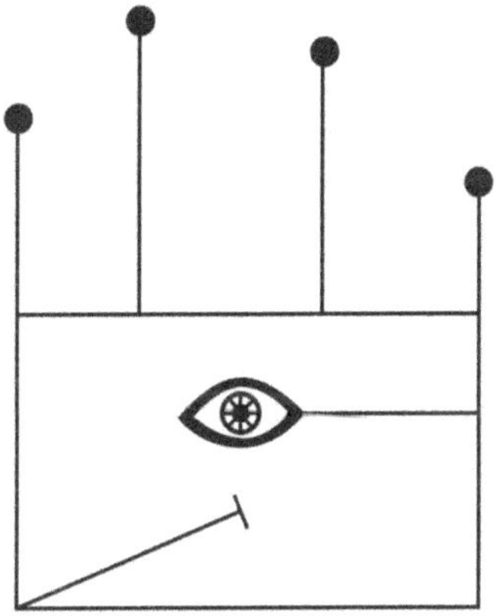

Blesu

Sign of Koth

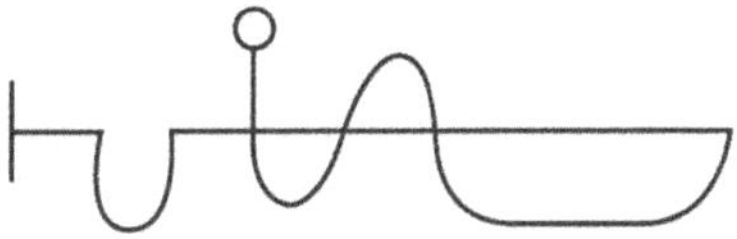

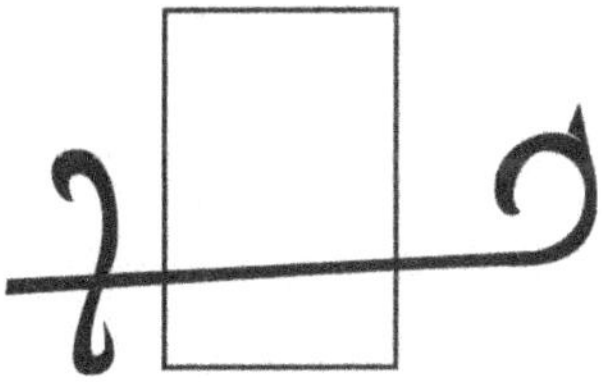

Kuthulhu

'Al Azif' Necronomicon - Wilson, Hay, Turner, Langford

Sigil Design from various editions of the Necronomicon

1 2 3 4 5 6 7 8 9
A B C D E F G H I
J K L M N O P Q R
S T U V W X Y Z &

G A B R I E L
7 1 2 9 9 5 3

Letter / Number Values

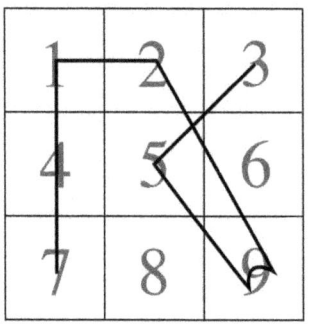

3 x 3 Magic Square

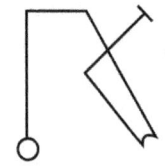

Sigil of Gabriel

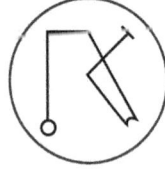 

Seal of Gabriel   Pentacle of Gabriel

Create a linear sigil and turn it into a seal and pentacle

SPIRIT SIGILS

Hebrew

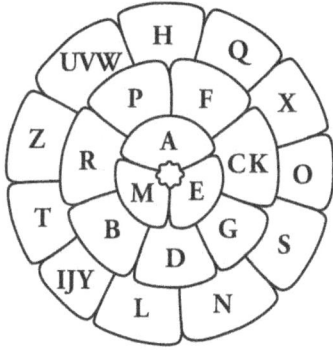

Enochian / English / Latin

Golden Dawn Rosy Cross Cipher (Double Star of the Sefer Yetzirah)

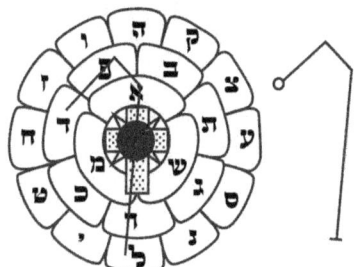

Hebrew. Raphael - correct

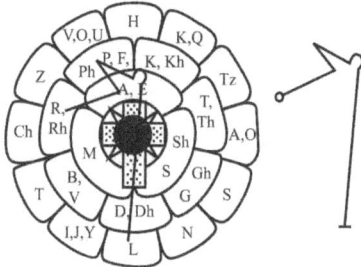

Latin. Raphael - incorrect

E	R	A	O	Y
V	F	S	B	K
L	W	G	P	C
Z	M	T	H	Q
D	X	N	U	IJ

Agrippa's 5x5 Kamea

Q	W	E	R	T
Y	U	IJ	O	P
A	S	D	F	G
H	K	L	Z	X
C	V	B	N	M

QWERT keyboard

Letter Cipher Squares

SIGILS, SEALS AND PENTACLES

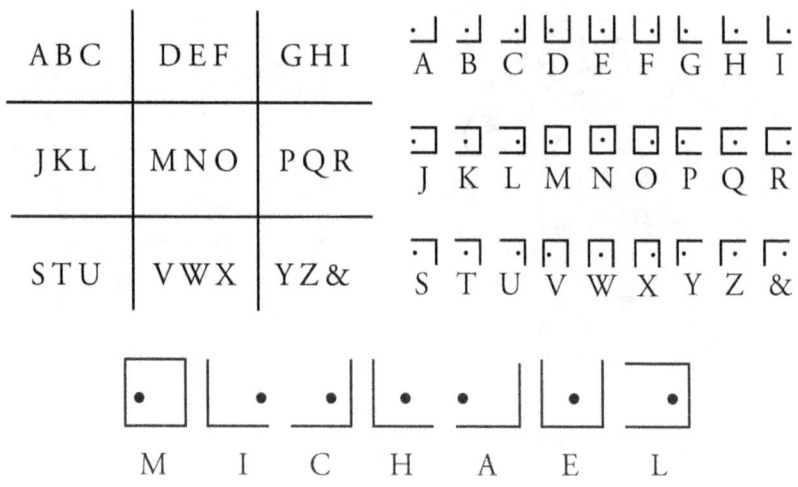

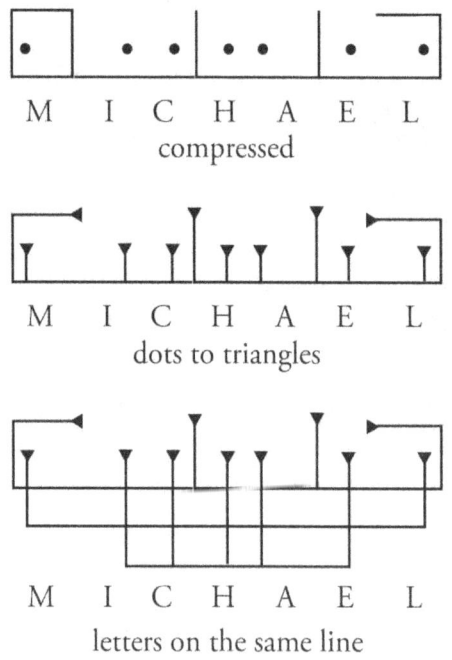

Rosicrucian Aiq Bkr or Nine Chambers Cipher

M I C H A E L
compressed

M I C H A E L
dots to triangles

M I C H A E L
letters on the same line

Olympian Sigil for Michael

SPIRIT SIGILS

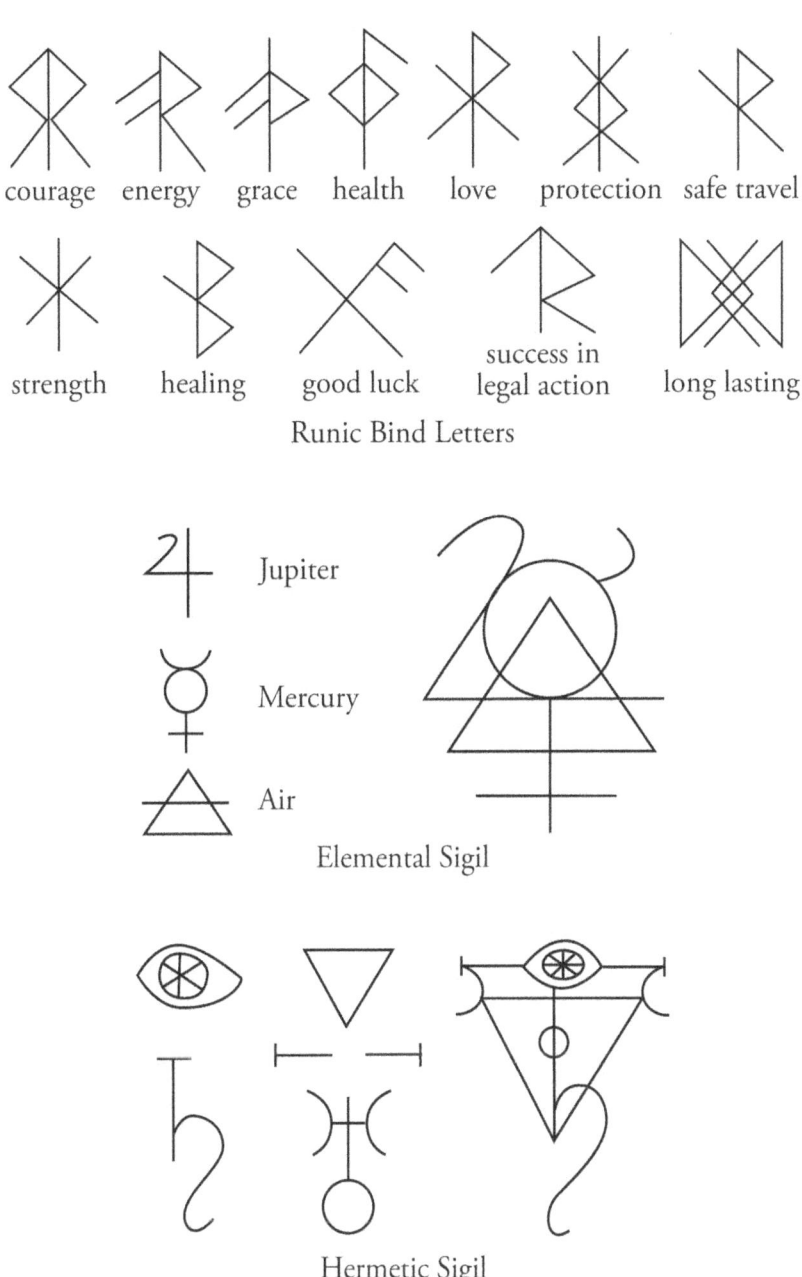

courage energy grace health love protection safe travel

strength healing good luck success in legal action long lasting

Runic Bind Letters

Jupiter

Mercury

Air

Elemental Sigil

Hermetic Sigil

Binding Letters and Symbols

SIGILS, SEALS AND PENTACLES

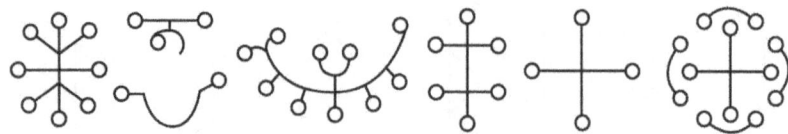

Protective spell written in Charakters from Coptic text

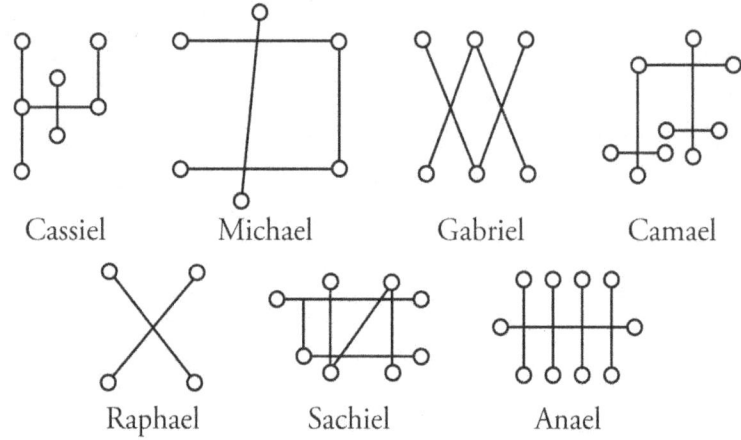

Celestial Sigils for the Archangels - Sefer Yetzirah

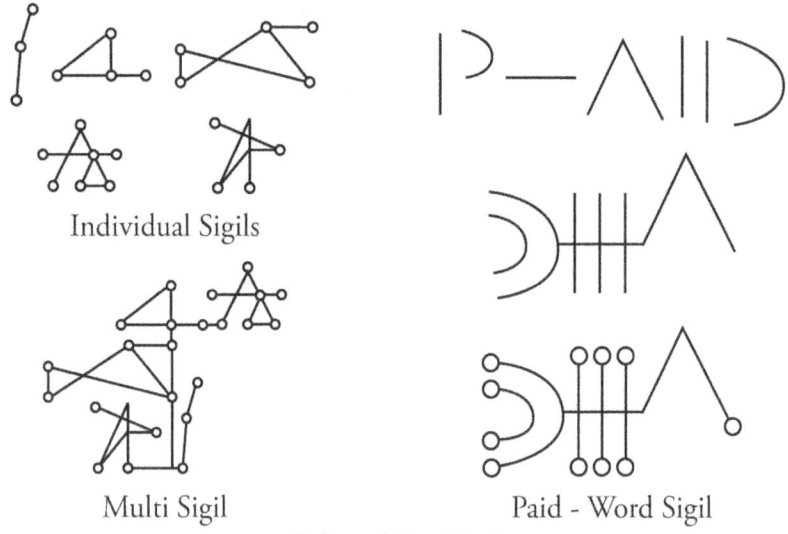

Multi Sigil   Paid - Word Sigil

Celestial Sigil Style

SPIRIT SIGILS

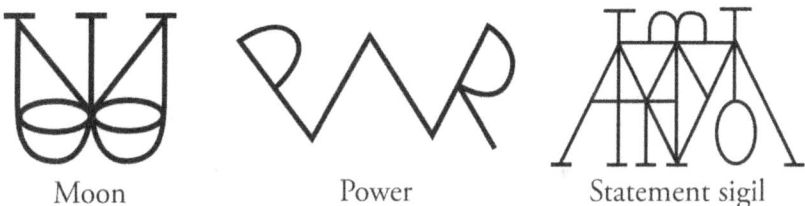

Moon — Power — Statement sigil

Austin Osman Spare's Sigilisation Technique

CHOSMGIK - Chaos Magick — Success

PAID£ — Beelzebub

Variation in Word Sigil Design

IWSHTOBANECRM — Rearranged to create a 'little picture'

"I wish to obtain the Necronomicon"

How to create a Statement sigil

Word and Statement Sigils

Spirit Seals

A spirit seal is a spirit's sigil placed in the center of a circle to create a seal which gives the sigil authority. This is done to make the sigil 'official' on behalf of the creator of the sigil. It is a more polished graphic representation of the spirit's sigil.

In ceremonial magic, seals are used to summon spirits, as they connect to a specific entity to help one with the work they are doing, in a similar manner to that of a sigil. The words 'seal' and 'sigil' are used interchangeably as they are both derived from the Latin 'sigillum' meaning 'signature', as both create or influence vibrations towards a specific desire or request.

Seals were in use from before Babylonian times, today they are most commonly known from the tradition of pressing an engraved metal 'seal' or 'signet ring' into red wax as a symbol of authority. This makes them powerful symbols, employed for all types of spiritual and magical workings, used to procure protection from evil spirits, venomous snakes, wounds, disease, death in battle, imprisonment and poverty amongst many other ills.

Such seals were commonly inscribed onto parchment or engraved into crystal to create amulets, or impressed on to a solid three-dimensional object such as clay, wax, wood or metal, to be worn as spiritual jewelry, to be carried and re-used as often as the owner choses. Their use and designs were circulated in magical and medical manuscripts. Seals were also copied onto amulet rolls which may have been multi-purpose or as a model from which single seals were copied onto smaller amulets.

Traditionally, seals were written on parchment with red ink which has been considered especially lucky since the invention of writing, when the names of deities and spirits were written in red to distinguish them from all other words.

To create a magic seal, first decide on the goal or intention and chose or create a seal that represents that goal then write the influence or request on the back of the seal. Strengthen the seal using a spirit oil, focusing on one's intention as one gently rubs the oil on the seal.

Once you have chosen a seal for the purpose, it can be activated in many different ways. It may be placed under a candle, inside a candle or tied to the outside of a candle. The seal can also be burnt in the candles flame. Seals can also be carved into larger candles such as Pull Out candles. This is especially good when trying to banish or get rid of something unwanted.

To attract love, wealth, good fortune or wisdom, anoint the seal with oil and carry it with you to attract what you desire. They can be placed in a bag with other seals, herbs, crystals or anything else, to enhance or raise the vibration of what you are trying to accomplish.

Seals are mainly circular but can be rectangular, triangular or oval in shape. Some are very simple, others are more complex, containing detailed amounts of esoteric knowledge represented by sigils, magic squares, planetary, alchemical and zodiac signs, elemental shapes, a picture or emblem and a motto, many with their intent or request written on the reverse. The seal may also bear the name of spirits written in Hebrew, Greek or Latin, or in a magic cipher like the Passing the River script.

Seals featured heavily in Judeo-Christian and Hebrew mysticism. In Judeo-Christian mysticism, the Seals of the Archangels have historically been used during magic rituals, as well as worn as a talisman for various purposes. The 17th century Book of Armadel, a French manuscript of celestial magic contains information, seals and sigils of angels, demons and other spirits. It was translated into English in 1890 by S L Mathers.

Seals of Solomon

The Seals of Solomon were developed in the western medieval occult traditions from Islamic and Jewish mysticism. The most recognizable of these seals is a hexagram in a circle, this is the design inscribed on the signet ring attributed to King Solomon. It is the predecessor to the Star of David, which became the symbol of the Jewish people in modern times. It was often depicted as either a pentagram or a hexagram shape, the hexagram became associated with Hebrew and Arabic mysticism and the pentagram with Western occultism, where it was also known as the Pentangle of Solomon.

There are several different forms of the Seal or Ring of Solomon but in its most basic form it consists of two interlocking equilateral triangles forming a six-pointed star. The upward pointing triangle is symbolic of Fire, the downward triangle of Water. In alchemy, it represents the seven planets and their metals. Made of gold or silver, this seal is to be held before the face of the exorcist to preserve him from the stinking sulphurous flames and flaming breath of evil spirits. Other forms of the Ring of Solomon include metal discs inscribed with the names of spirits.

The ring mainly gave Solomon the power to command demons, genies and spirits or to speak to animals. Due to the proverbial wisdom of Solomon, his ring or its design came to be seen as an amulet or talisman in Renaissance magic and drawing.

The Ring of Solomon figures prominently in the Treatise of Solomon but is conspicuously absent from the (Greater) Key of Solomon. Although it is mentioned in one of the conjurations of the Lesser Key of Solomon, the ring, its construction and use is otherwise not mentioned.

The Seals of Solomon is also used as an umbrella term given to the seals, pentagrams and hexagrams used in the goetic ritual of the Lesser Keys of Solomon. The Hexagram of Solomon is a figure to be made on calf skin parchment and worn on the shirt of one's white vestments and covered with linen cloth, white and pure, which is to be shown to the spirits when they appear, so that they may be compelled to take human shape upon them and be obedient.

The Pentagram of Solomon is a seal is to be made in gold or silver and worn upon the breast, having the seal of the spirit on the reverse. It is to preserve the possessor from danger and command the spirits.

The Secret Seal of Solomon is a bronze seal used by King Solomon to bind and seal the demons and their legions within the Vessel of Brass. In doing this, he gained the love of all manner of persons and overcame in battle, for neither weapons, nor fire, nor water could hurt him.

The Magic Disc of Solomon is made from gold or silver and held before the face of the exorcist to preserve him from the sulphurous smell and fiery breath of evil spirits.

The Seals of the Spirits are the sigils of the 72 demonic spirits of the Ars Goetia of the Lesser Key of Solomon, summoned by Solomon to build his temple. They correspond numerically to the 72 Angels of the Shemhamphorash, who provide protection to the magician from their evil countenance. The Seals of the Angels of the Zodiac are from the Ars Theugria Goetia of the Lesser Key of Solomon.

Seal of Ameth, Sigillum Dei Aemeth

The Seal of the Truth of God is most widely known from the work of Dr. John Dee, the 16th century court astrologer to Queen Elizabeth 1. While the seal does appear in older texts of which Dee was probably familiar, he was not happy with them and ultimately claimed guidance from angels in constructing his version, inscribing the seal onto a circular bee's wax tablet.

Dee's system of Angel magic known as Enochian, is heavily rooted in the number 7 which is strongly connected with the seven planets of astrology. As such, the Seal of Ameth is primarily constructed of heptagrams or seven pointed stars and heptagons or seven sided polygons.

On the reverse, Dee created the word 'AGLA', an abbreviation for a Latin phrase that translates as 'The Lord is Mighty Forever'. It is used as an amulet in its own right.

Seals of the Four Elementary Spirits of the Watchtowers

In Enochian ritual, the Watchtowers represent the four cardinal points or four quarters, North, South, East and West. They are also associated with the four elements, Fire, Water, Air, Earth. The seals are used to call upon the aid of angels ruling over the four directions and invoked during ritual of casting a magic circle.

The Watchtowers stand guard over the material universe and are responsible for maintaining and governing it. From ancient times, the Universe was believed to stretch outwardly toward the four directions and to be composed inwardly of the four elements. The four elements were believed to be the building blocks of Creation.

Ameth Seals (Enochian Pentacles)

The Enochian names of the seven Archangels are found on the outer ring of the Seal of Ameth. Their names and seals were published by Dee in the Black Venus grimoire. Dee connected the Ameth Angels to the Black Venus and Olympic spirits, and to the seven planets, seven days of the week and the seven Archangels. Enochian seals are powerful talismans used to bind demons, protect an area from angel's interference and conceal humans from every angel in creation.

Hebrew Seals

Many Hebrew seals appear in the western occult tradition, introduced through the Sefer Raziel and transmitted among other grimoires such as the 6th and 7th Books of Moses, that first appeared in inexpensive pamphlets published in 18th century Germany. Allegedly written by Moses and passed on as lost books of the Hebrew Bible, they contain incantations, spells and seals to help the operator perform various tasks from controlling the weather and people, to contacting the dead or biblical religious figures.

Seals of the Sages of the Pyramids

As well as sigils, symbols and names, seal design employs metaphoric images, pictures or illustrations that alchemically encode information. The introduction of alchemic metaphor into seal design began in the 12th century with the Smaradgina Tabula, a pictorial representation of the short alchemical text known as the Emerald Tablet, attributed to the legendary Hermes Trimegistus, alleged author of hundreds of treatises on astrology, alchemy and magic.

In the text, the reader is introduced into the classic Hermetic formulation "As Above, So Below", to the notion that the sought-for god of the alchemical 'Operation of the Sun', be that the Elixir or Philosopher's Stone, as for example, the Sun as its Father, the Moon as its Mother and the Earth as its Nurse. Such opaque, poetic language was to represent a major style of transmission of the occult science of alchemy from the Middle Ages into the Renaissance and beyond.

Many Medieval and Renaissance authors made use of cover images to conceal the identity of the substances and processes employed in the Great Work. Hence, Quicksilver would become the 'drago' or simply speak of 'necessary water'. Volatile salts became Eagles with bows in their talons, Colour changes would be implied by black ravens and white swans, golden eagles and multicoloured peacocks

Given the highly visual nature of alchemical metaphor, it was only a matter of time before the emergence of a new genre of alchemical imagery influenced not only the magical design of the Seals of the Sages of the Pyramids but also the masonic Great Seal of the United States of America.

Replete with magical and alchemic metaphor, the Seals of the Sages of the Pyramids were first published in the Black Pullet, a 17th century French grimoire along with its signet ring and the characters engraved upon it. These secret seals are said to comprise the Science of Magical Talismans, the Art of Necromancy and of the Cabala, giving the magician the acquisition of power to command all beings and to unmask all science and bewitchments.

Seals of the 'Simon' Necronomicon
Examples of more recent powerful seals can be found in the postmodern grimoire the 'Simon' Necronomicon. The front cover features a seal designed by Khem Gaigan known as either the Call of Cthuthulhu or the Sigil of the Gate. Based on Golden Dawn magical squares, the seal is composed of three sigils contained in a circle, the sigils are ancient signs carved in the grey stone that was the Gateway to the Outside, but it is not a Gate.

As a positive symbol of protection, the seal is used in the normal invocation of the Watcher which is made in the course of any normal ceremony when it is necessary to summon the Watcher to preside over the outer perimeter of the circle or gate.

Of the three sigils, the first is the sign of our Race from beyond the stars and is called ARRA. It is the sigil of the covenant with the Elder Gods which must be worn at all times by your Race. The second is the Elder sign called AGGA and is the key whereby the Power of the Elder Gods may be summoned and thou shalt wear at all times. The third sign is the Sigil of the Watcher called BANDAR. The Watchers are a race sent by the Elders Ones to keep a vigil while one sleeps.

To be effective, these seals must be graven on stone and set in the ground or set upon the alter of offerings, or carried to the Rock of Invocations or engraved on the metal of one's God or Goddess and hung about the neck but hidden from the view of the profane. Of the three sigils, ARRA and AGGA may be used separately and singly and alone. The BANDAR must never be used alone but with one or both of the others.

The 'Simon' Necronomicon also features a set of seals that take their inspiration from the 50 names of the Sumerian God Marduk, whose story is told in the epic of the Enuma Elish. They appear in the chapter titled the Book of 50 Names of Marduk.

The Seals of the Zonei are 7 square, planetary amulets denoting that the Gods of the Stars are 7. They have 7 seals, each of which may be used in their turn. They have 7 colours, 7 essences and each is a separate step on the Ladder of Lights. They are approached by 7 Gates, each of which may be used in their turn.

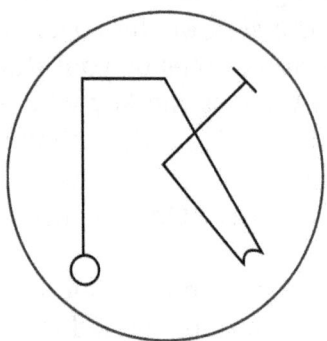 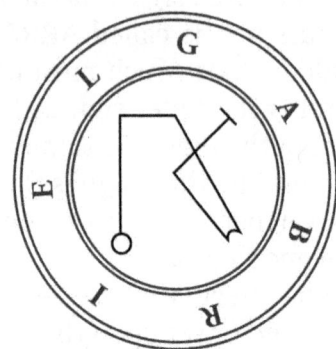

Seal of Gabriel　　　　Polished / Perfected Seal

Seal of Aral the Angel of Fire

Center
Zodiac Fire Signs - Sagittarius, Leo, Aries

Bottom
Michael - Archangel of Fire and the South

Outer
Aral - Ruling Angel of Fire and the North

SPIRIT SEALS

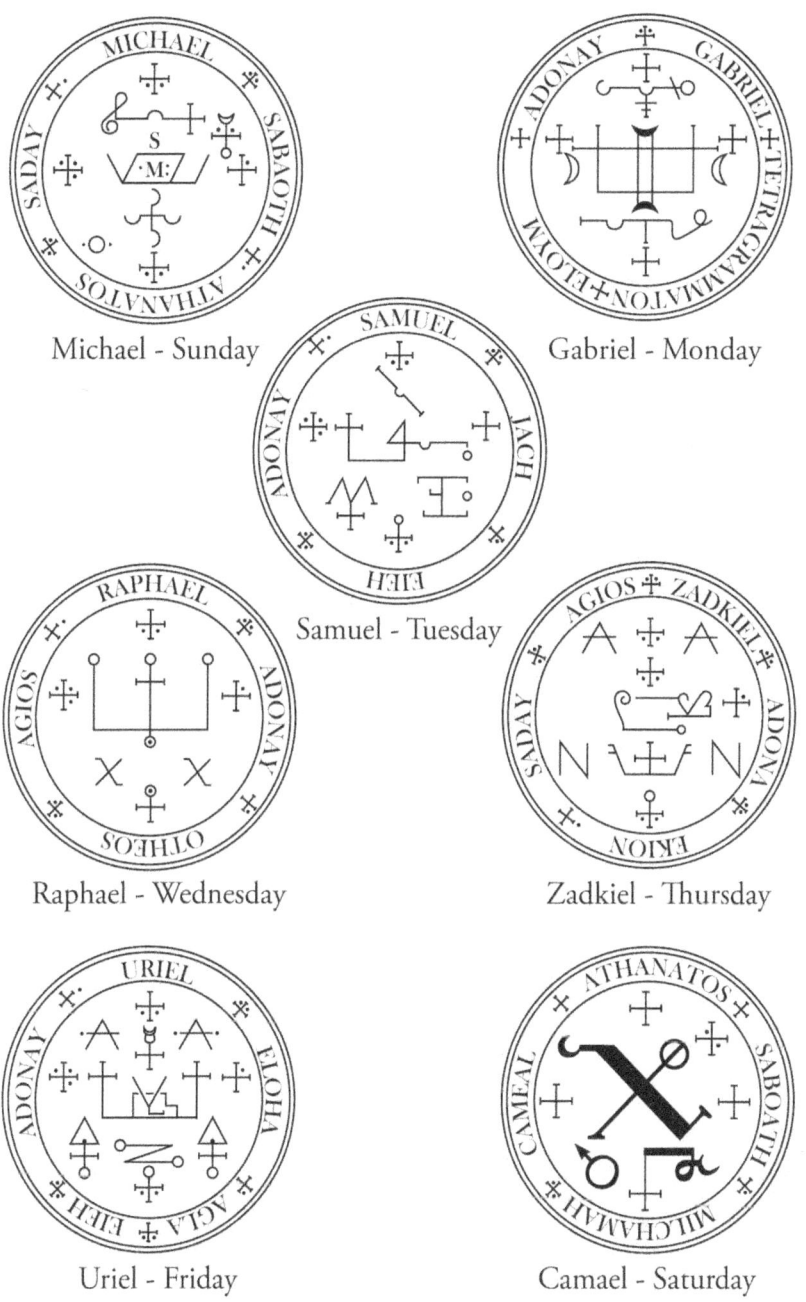

Michael - Sunday
Gabriel - Monday
Samuel - Tuesday
Raphael - Wednesday
Zadkiel - Thursday
Uriel - Friday
Camael - Saturday

Seals of the Archangels - Book of Abramelin

SIGILS, SEALS AND PENTACLES

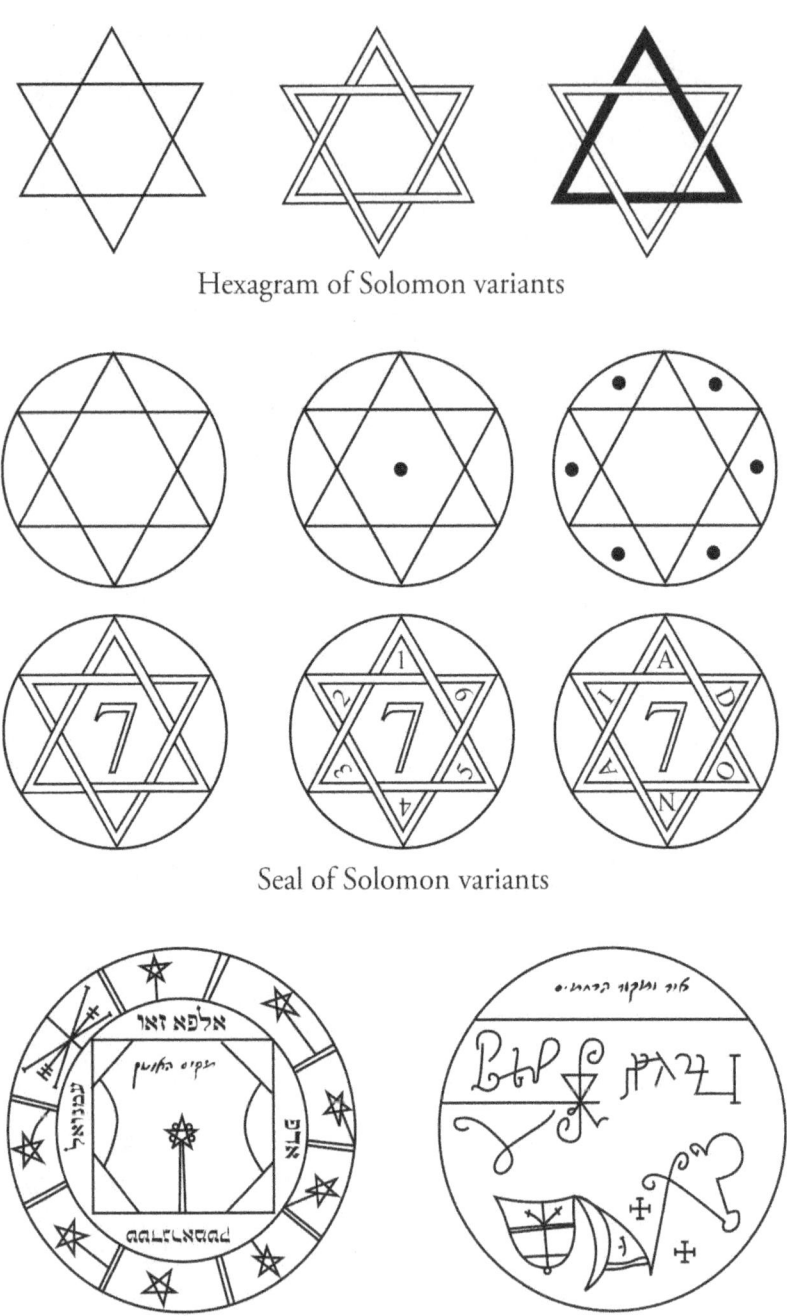

Hexagram of Solomon variants

Seal of Solomon variants

Solomonic Seals from 5th / 6th c. Hebrew Manuscripts

SPIRIT SEALS

Solomonic Seals - 15th c. Greek manuscript

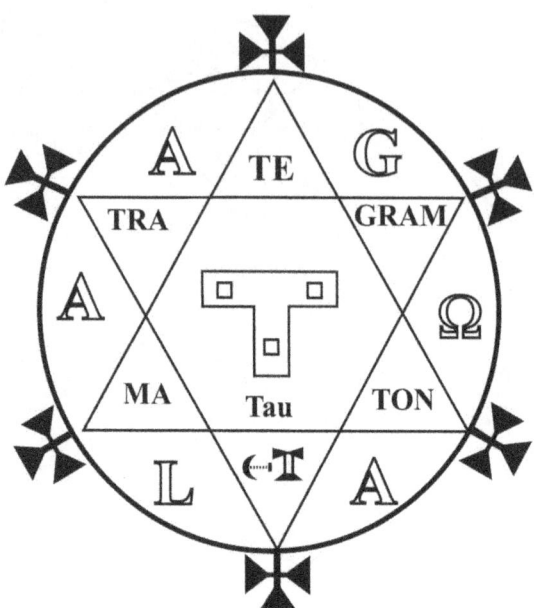

Hexagram of Solomon

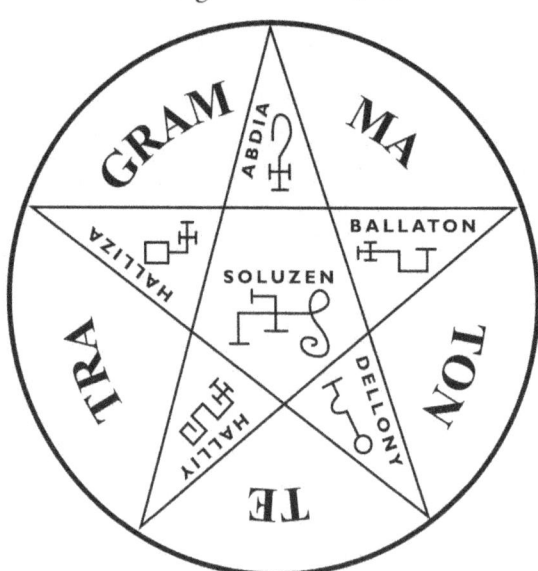

Pentagram of Solomon

Seals of Solomon - Lesser Key of Solomon / Ars Goetia

SPIRIT SEALS

Secret Seal of Solomon

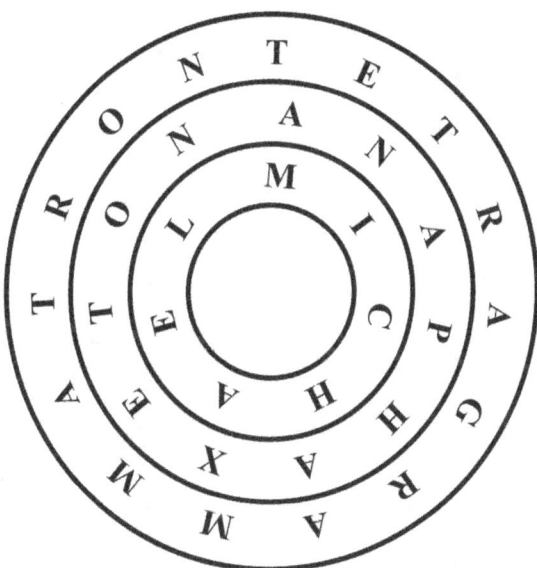

Magic Ring or Disc of Solomon

Seals of Solomon - Lesser Key of Solomon / Ars Goetia

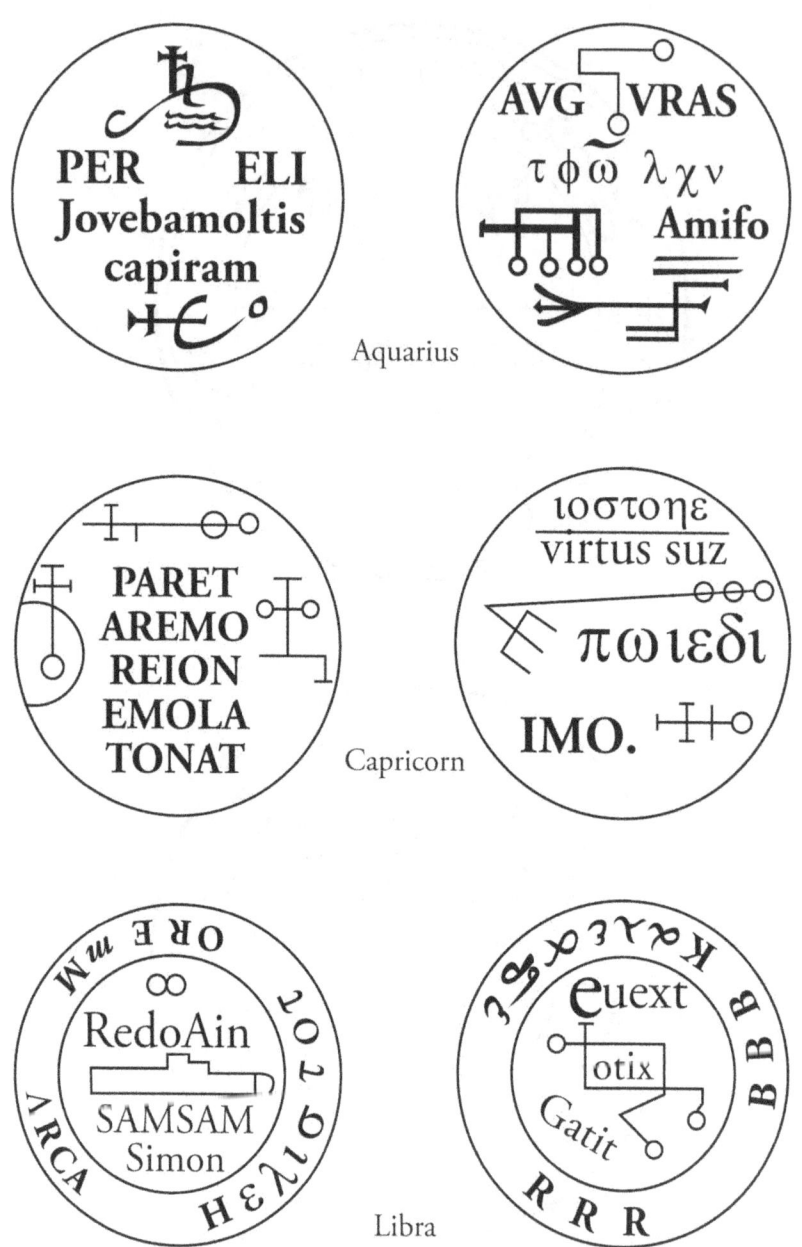

Seals of the Angels of the Zodiac
Lesser Key of Solomon / Ars Pauline

Seals of the Angels of the Zodiac
Lesser Keys of Solomon / Ars Pauline

Front

Sigillum Dei Aemeth / Seal of Ameth / Seal of the Truth of God

SPIRIT SEALS

Reverse

AGLA / Seal of Ameth

Element - Fire
Direction - South
Name - O HEOOAA A TAN

Element - Air
Direction - East
Name - TA HAOEL OG

Element - Water
Direction - West
Name - THA HE BY O A AT NUN

Element - Earth
Direction - North
Name - THA HAA OTH E

Seals of the Four Enochian Watchers

SPIRIT SEALS

AAOTH - Michael
Sunday, Sun

GALETHOG - Gabriel
Monday, Moon

INNON - Samuel
Tuesday, Mars

THAOTH - Raphael
Wednesday, Mercury

HORLWYN - Sachiel
Thursday, Jupiter

GALAS - Anniel
Friday, Venus

GETHOG - Cathiel
Saturday, Saturn

Enochian Ameth Seals of the Angels of the Days of the Week

Spirit of Fire - 6th Book of Moses

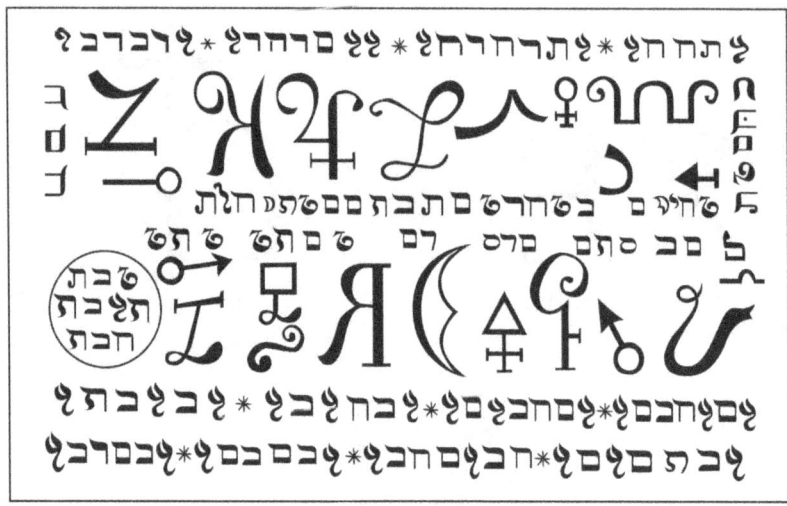

Spirit of Fire - 7th Book of Moses

Hebrew Seals

SPIRIT SEALS

Smaragdina Tablet / Emerald Tablet

Great Seal of the United States of America

Alchemical Metaphor

Seals of the Sages of the Pyrimids - Black Pullet

SPIRIT SEALS

Seals of the Sages of the Pyrimids - Black Pullet

Seals of the Sages of the Pyrimids - Black Pullet

SPIRIT SEALS

Seals of the Sages of the Pyrimids - Black Pullet

SIGILS, SEALS AND PENTACLES

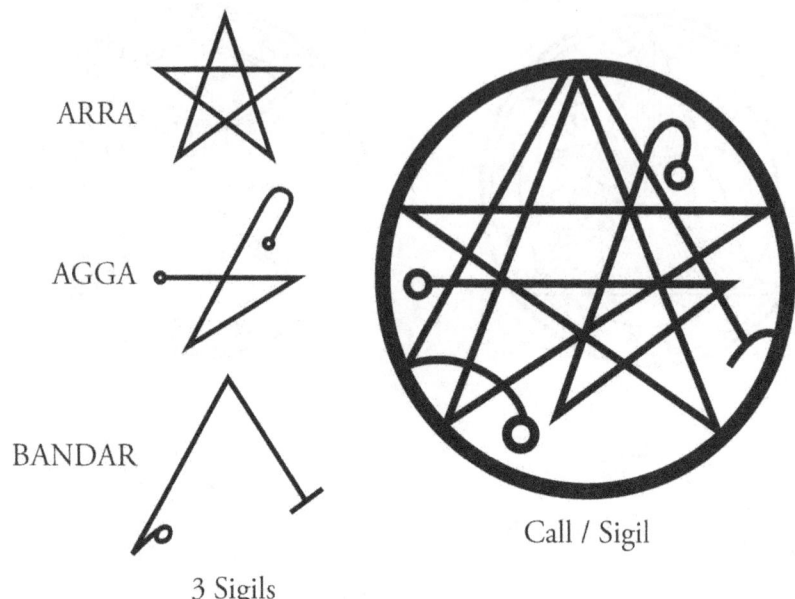

3 Sigils

Call of Cthuthulhu / Sigil of the Gateway

Some of the Fifty Seals and Epithets of Marduk

Seals from the 'Simon' Necronomicon

SPIRIT SEALS

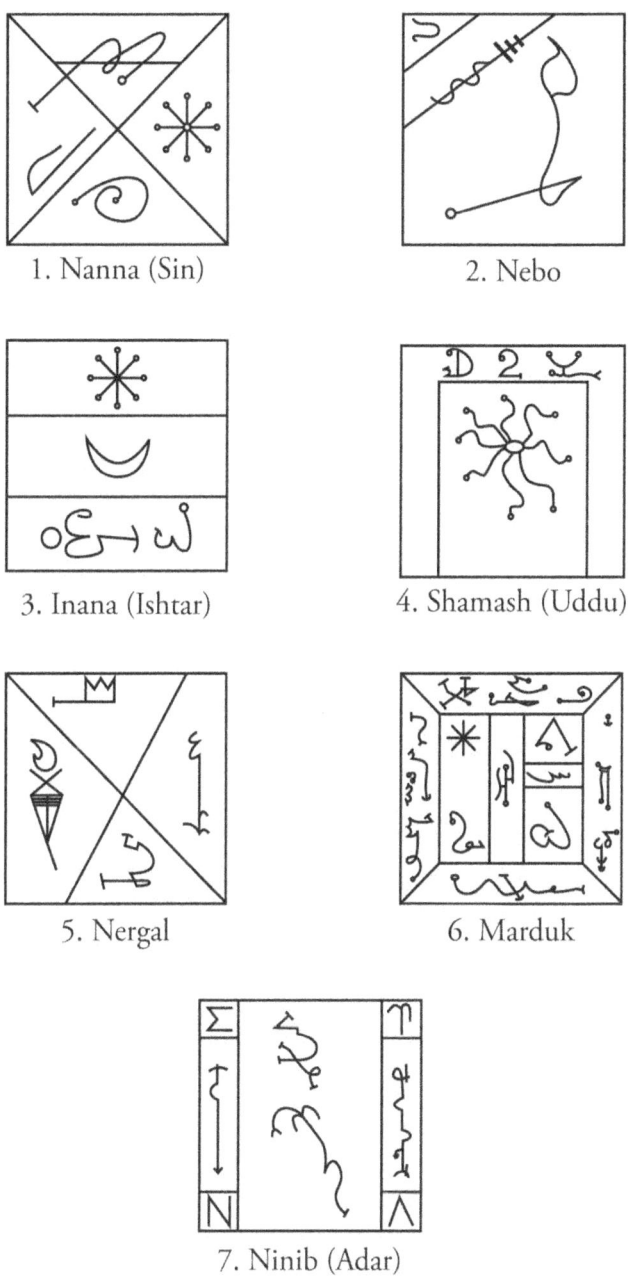

1. Nanna (Sin)
2. Nebo
3. Inana (Ishtar)
4. Shamash (Uddu)
5. Nergal
6. Marduk
7. Ninib (Adar)

Seals of the Seven Zonei - 'Simon' Necronomicon

Pentagrams and Pentacles

A pentacle is a flat talisman made of parchment, sheet metal or other substance, marked with a magic symbol or symbols such as a pentagram or a hexagram. When used in magical evocation it is synonymous with the sigil.

In magic practice, the term pentacle is often used to denote a pentagram or five-pointed star because pentagrams were often used in the preparation of pentacles, although more often than not they feature hexagrams rather than pentagrams. In extended use, pentagram and pentacle are treated as distinct, generally pentagrams are worn as amulets, pentacles are worn as talismans.

Amulets are small objects worn to ward off evil, harm, or illness or to bring good fortune, a protective charm. Talisman's may be a stone, ring, or other object, engraved with figures or characters supposed to possess occult powers and worn as an amulet or charm.

Pentagrams

In paganism, the pentacle is synonymous with the pentagram, a symbol that has been around since the stone age, revered by almost all ancient cultures. The symbol itself is a five-pointed star whose lines intersect each other at five different points. Its modern use is descended from the western occult tradition. Occultist's have largely associated the pentagram with the magic numerology contained in the number 5, the five physical senses – sight, hearing, touch, smell, taste. The five elements of spirit, fire, air, water, earth, and humanity and the human body represented by four outstretched limbs and head.

A pentagram can be orientated with the single point pointing upwards, or in reverse with the single point pointing downwards. This gives different meanings to each pentagram, 19th century groups such as the Golden Dawn held that the point-up pentagram represents the rulership of spirit over matter or physical elements, while a point-down pentagram represents the descent of spirit into matter or matter subsuming spirit. It is largely this interpretation that led to the religion of Wicca adopting the point up pentagram and Satanism the point down pentagram as their representative symbols.

In his text, Transcendental Magic, the 19th occultist Eliphas Levi describes their orientation thus *"It is initiation or profomation, it is Lucifer or Vespar, the Star of the Morning or Evening. It is Mary or Lilith, victory or death, day or night. The pentagram with the points in the descendent represents Satan as the Goat of the Sabbath, when one point is on the ascendant it is a sign of the Saviour. With the two ascending points and one descending point we may see the horns, ears and beard of the Goat of Mendes, when it becomes the sign of infernal evocations"*.

The pentagram is generally expressed as male and female, in order to generate a greater whole. For example, Wiccan's see the pentagram as representing the Triple Goddess with three of the points representing the three phases of the moon, waxing, full and waning, and the Horned God with two of the points representing two horns or his dual light and dark nature's. Agrippa speaks of the number 5 as generally representing the union of male and female as the sum of two and three with two representing the Mother and three representing the Father. A double pentagram may represent the union of opposites.

In ritual magic, the pentagram is commonly accepted as a symbol of protection and exorcism, drawing away evil and other unwanted energies and entities. In ceremonial magic, the pentagram is most commonly found when placed within a circle, in which the magician stands for protection from the spirit during evocation.

Various pentagram designs have been developed over the centuries. Agrippa depicted the Pythagorean pentagram as an example of a divinity revealed symbol, as revealed to Antiochus Soteris. The Pythagorean's used the symbol to represent themselves and it was used as an amulet. The letters round the outside starting at the top and moving clockwise are U G I EI A, which is Greek for 'health'. Later similar amulets would be created with the letters S A L I S which is Latin for 'health'.

The Samael and Lilith design is the first known pentagram/goat head combination. Published by Stanislas de Guaite in La Clef de la Magie in 1897. It is the primary influence for the Baphomet Pentagram, the official symbol of the Church of Satan. The five Hebrew letters spell out the name Leviathan, a symbol of the abyss and hidden truth. Leviathan is the connection between the demon Samael and the demoness Lilith.

The 19th century pentagram constructed by occultist Eliphas Levi is commonly interpreted as a symbol of mankind, as many pentagrams are. However, it is a symbol of many things that unite in the existence of mankind, as is evidenced in the variety of additional symbols involved.

The Gardnerian Pentagram was devised by Gerald Gardner, a founder of the Wiccan religion. It is a circular disc bearing seven symbols surrounding a central pentagram. The top left downward triangle represents the first degree of initiation/elevation in Wicca. The top right reverse pentagram represents the second degree. The central upward triangle in combination with the central pentagram represents the third degree. The third-degree Wiccan Pentacle is used exclusively by traditional Wiccans practicing the third-degree system of elevation, the highest rank attainable.

In the lower half, the figure on the left is the Horned God, while the back to back crescents are the Moon Goddess. The SS at the bottom represents the dichotomy of mercy and severity or the kiss and the scourge.

The Lightning Bolt pentagram was the personal symbol of Anton LeVey, founder of the Church of Satan. The bolt represents the flash of inspiration that drives people to greatness. Theistic Satanist's also use the symbol to represent power and life force descending from Satan into matter.

Pentacle

Pentacles are flat talismans upon which a magical design is drawn and sometimes on the reverse. Usually disk shaped, pentacles can be square, triangular, oval or diamond in shape. They are made from paper or cloth in two dimensions and in metal in three dimensions, and inscribed with a magic symbol or symbols.

Symbols may include star shapes, the most common being the pentagram, hexagram or other polygons. Many have no geometric forms and employ sigils, illustrations, names of spirits, planetary symbols and the signs of the zodiac.

Agrippa said pentacles were used to *"know all future things and command the whole of nature, have the power over devils and angels and do miracles"*.

There are various origins and definitions for the word 'pentacle'. The word pentacle has its origins in the Latin word 'pentaculum' meaning 'little painting'. It usually refers to the complex diagrams that were inscribed on the ground by magicians as protective circles. Alternatively, the word pentacle comes from the French meaning 'hangs from the neck', providing protection and authority. In Renaissance France, pentacle was used to refer to any talisman. During the 19th century, the occultist Eliphas Levi wrote the word as 'pantacle', a trend continued by Aleister Crowley in the 20th century.

In the Golden Dawn system of the 20th century, pentacles are not worn around the neck but wrapped in a cloth covering for the magician to wear fastened to the breast as a Lamen.

Pentacles are Holy signs protecting the wearer from evil choices and events, and helping and assisting to bind, exterminate and drive away evil spirits and allure the good spirits, reconciling them to the wearer. These pentacles are composed of either Characters of the Good Spirits of the superior order, or of sacred pictures of the Holy letters or revelations, apt and fit versides, which are composed of geometric figures and Holy Names of God.

The useful characters to make the pentacles are the characters of the good spirits of the first, second and maybe the third order and must be drawn in a double circle with the name of their angel and add a divine name comparable to their spirit and office.

The first pentacle was depicted in the 16th century grimoire called the Heptameron. It is made up of a hexagon, a cross and various letters.

Pentacles of Solomon

The most famous pentacles are the Pentacles of Solomon, a range of magical designs published in the 16th century grimoire, the Key of Solomon. They are those sets of astrological and planetary talismans known as the Holy Pentacles or Planetary Medals.

Solomon was given the keys as a set of pentacles, revealed to him by angels for the creation of talismans for use in everyday life. They offer supreme protection, made for the purpose of striking terror into the spirit, reducing them to obedience.

Each of the seven planets has a number of pentacles and a colour attributed to it. They are 7 Black Pentacles of Saturn. 7 Blue Pentacles of Jupiter. 7 Red Pentacles of Mars. 7 Yellow Pentacles of the Sun. 5 Green Pentacles of Venus. 5 Mixed Colour Pentacles of Mercury. 6 Silver/Grey Pentacles of the Moon. The first pentacle of the Moon is the only square pentacle. Each set of pentacles is consecrated to the angels which rule the planets. Since each planet rules in certain specific matters, an appropriate seal can be found to influence one's special situation or objective.

Used for invoking the spirits of the planets, their order is Saturn, Jupiter, Mars, Sun, Venus, Mercury, Moon. The pentacles are made from the appropriate planetary metal and the majority of the holy names used on the pentacles can be found in the grimoire called the Tablets of Moses.

The pentacles are seen as the greatest puzzle in the Key of Solomon. Their order varies widely from manuscript to manuscript. The oldest manuscripts only identify some of them, with later attempts made in later manuscripts to identify the rest with a planet too.

The Key of Solomon also includes the Mystical Seal of Solomon and the Great or Grand Pentacle of Solomon. The Mystical Seal or Figure of Solomon is shown on the frontispiece. The Grand Pentacle of Solomon is taken from the 1547 grimoire the Hepatmeron, this seal contains all the knowledge needed to perform Solomonic ceremonial magic. It serves to convene all spirits, when shown to them they will bow and obey the magician. It should be written on sheepskin or virgin parchment, tinted green. It contains all the knowledge needed to perform Solomonic magic. Both of which impart the mechanisms and requirements for the evocation of spirits and demons.

The pentacles are not the work of a single magician but influenced by the work of many magicians and many cultures across the great span of history, taken from earlier Arabic, Hebrew and Greek sources. Later traditions adopted them into their own practices, as many are clearly later inventions based on Agrippa and other sources.

Gates

The pentacle is a species of hieroglyphic representation of a 'gate' or 'door'. The word 'gate' can mean 'entrance, beginning' or 'a going in'. A gate is an access point into a person's life, where entry and exit of things are controlled. Gates are based on planetary practices, they are two-way, in or out of worlds, both angels and demons use gates to travel between realms. All gates are protected by a Watchtower and a Watcher, or Keeper of the Watch.

The ancient Egyptians believed that in the underworld there were various gates, doors and pylons, crossed every night by the Solar Boat of Ra and by the souls directed to the world of the dead. In their literature, the Book of Gates describes twelve gates or pylons of the underworld and in spite of being imagined as architecture, the gates were individually named as goddesses. The Book of the Dead mentions seven gates, each with its own god, doorkeeper and herald, for example, the seventh gate is guarded by the god 'Sharpest of the All', by the doorkeeper 'Straight of Voice' and the herald ' Rejecter of Rebels'.

Other funerary texts mention twenty-one secret portals of the 'Mansion of Osiris' in the 'Field of Reeds' with their own names and epithets and protected by two hundred anthropomorphic deities often depicted crouching on the ground holding large, threatening knives. The names of these 'feminine' entities can be as disturbing as the fourteenth gate – Mistress of Anger – Dancing on Blood, or harmless like the third gate, Mistress of the Alter. The guardian gods too were given names that inspired terror and above all, evoked their fearful powers, for example, 'Swallower of Sinner's' and 'Existing on Maggots'.

These themes are continued in those postmodern grimoires concerned with H P Lovecraft's Cthuthulhu Mythos. The 'Simon' Necronomicon explores the Sumerian mythology and magical rites that were just being discovered during Lovecraft's lifetime. It is from this that a connection with Aleister Crowley has been made, although the two never met, they are both considered to be on the 'same plane' concerning their interest in Sumerian ritual and demonology.

In the 'Simon' Necronomicon, the Gates refer to the process of self-initiation contained in it. Some say they are made up, others believe that they are based on the western occult tradition taken from the Qlipothic mysticism of Hebrew Cabala, that perfectly align them with the traditions of the ancients, *"the ancients believed that in order for one to be initiated, they must walk through the path of the dead while alive and through this experience, a 'transformation' occurs"*.

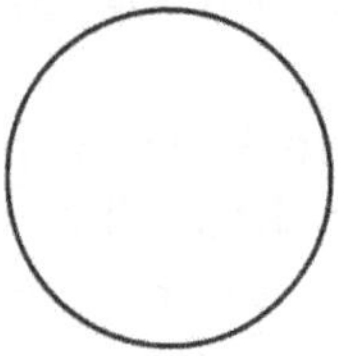

SIGILS, SEALS AND PENTACLES

Circle
continuous

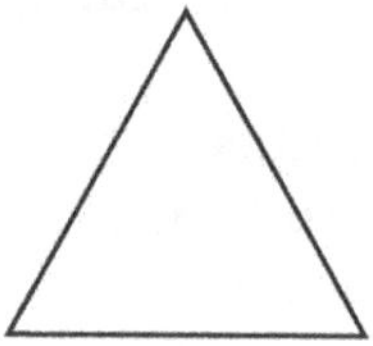

Triangle
continuous

Square
continuous

Pentagram
continuous

Pentagram
continuous

Heptagram
two triangles

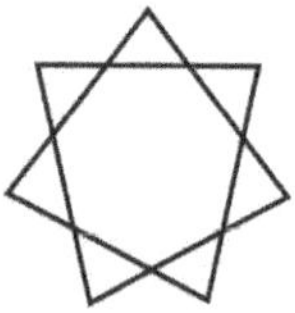

Heptagram
continuos

Heptagram
continuous

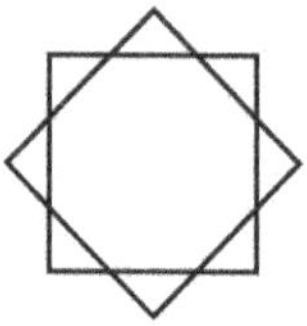

Octogram
two squares

Octogram
continuous

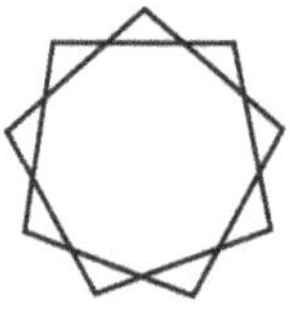

Enneagram
continuous

Enneagram
three triangles

Enneagram
continuous

PENTAGRAMS AND PENTACLES

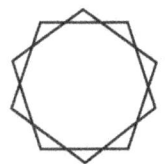
Dekagram
two pentagons

Dekagram
continuous

Dekagram
two pentagrams

Endekagram
continuous

Endekagram
continuous

Endekagram
continuous

Endekagram
continuous

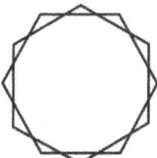
Dodekagram
two hexagons

Dodekagram
three squares

Dodekagram
four triangles

Dodekagram
continuous

Star / Pentacle Forms

SIGILS, SEALS AND PENTACLES

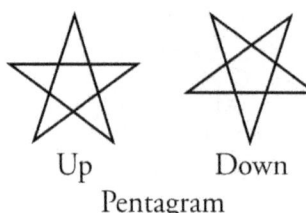

Up   Down
Pentagram

Pythagorean Pentagram
Agrippa

Samael & Lilith Pentagram

Tetragrammaton Pentagram
Eliphas Levi

Gardeners Pentagram
Wicca

3rd Degree
Wicca

Lighten Bolt Pentagram
Anton LeVey

Pentagram Design

PENTAGRAMS AND PENTACLES

Pentacle

Tarot Pentacle

Western Pentacle

Eastern Pentacle

Wiccan Pentacle
Female

Satanic Pentacle
Male

10 Pointed Star
Unity of the Sexes

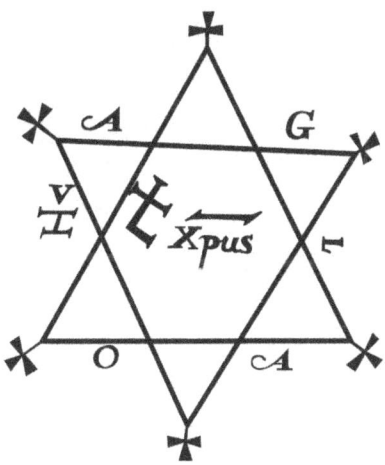
Heptameron Pentacle

Pentacle Design

SIGILS, SEALS AND PENTACLES

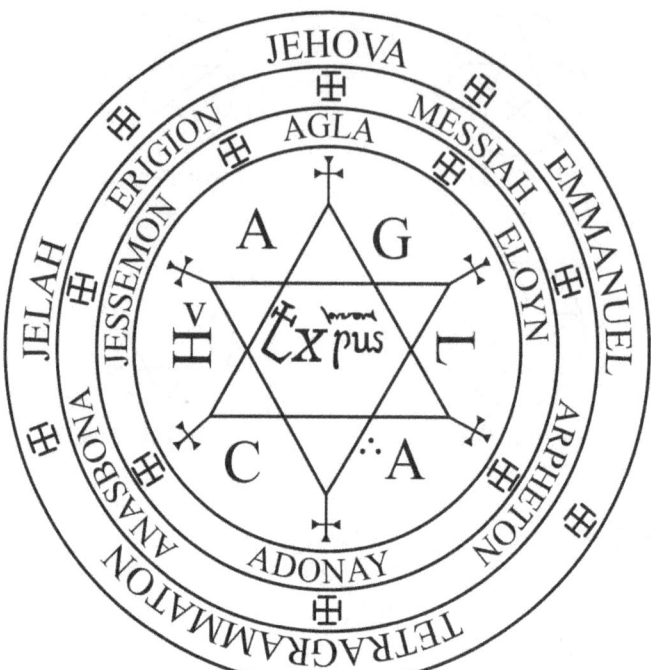

Great / Grand Pentacle of Solomom

Mystical Figure of Solomon

Pentacles of Solomon - (Greater) Key of Solomon

PENTAGRAMS AND PENTACLES

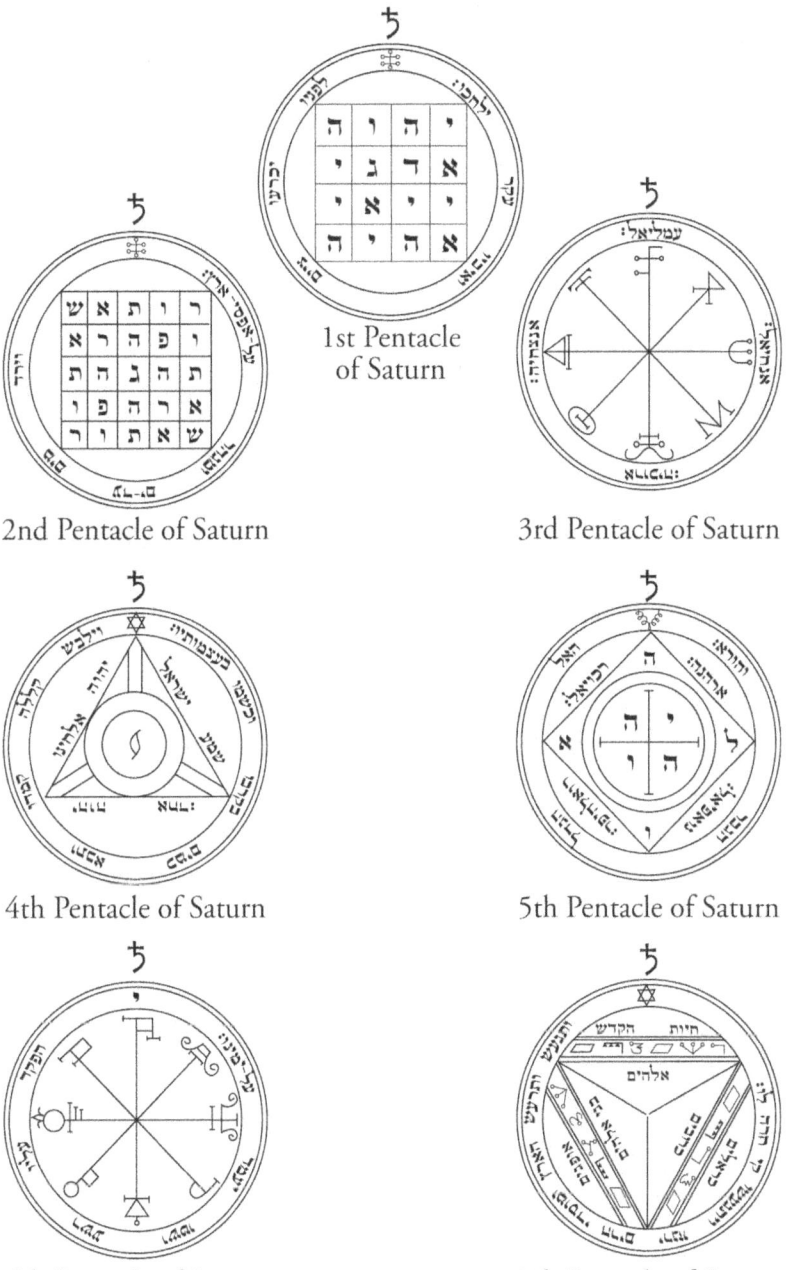

1st Pentacle of Saturn

2nd Pentacle of Saturn

3rd Pentacle of Saturn

4th Pentacle of Saturn

5th Pentacle of Saturn

6th Pentacle of Saturn

7th Pentacle of Saturn

Pentacles of Saturn - (Greater) Key of Solomon

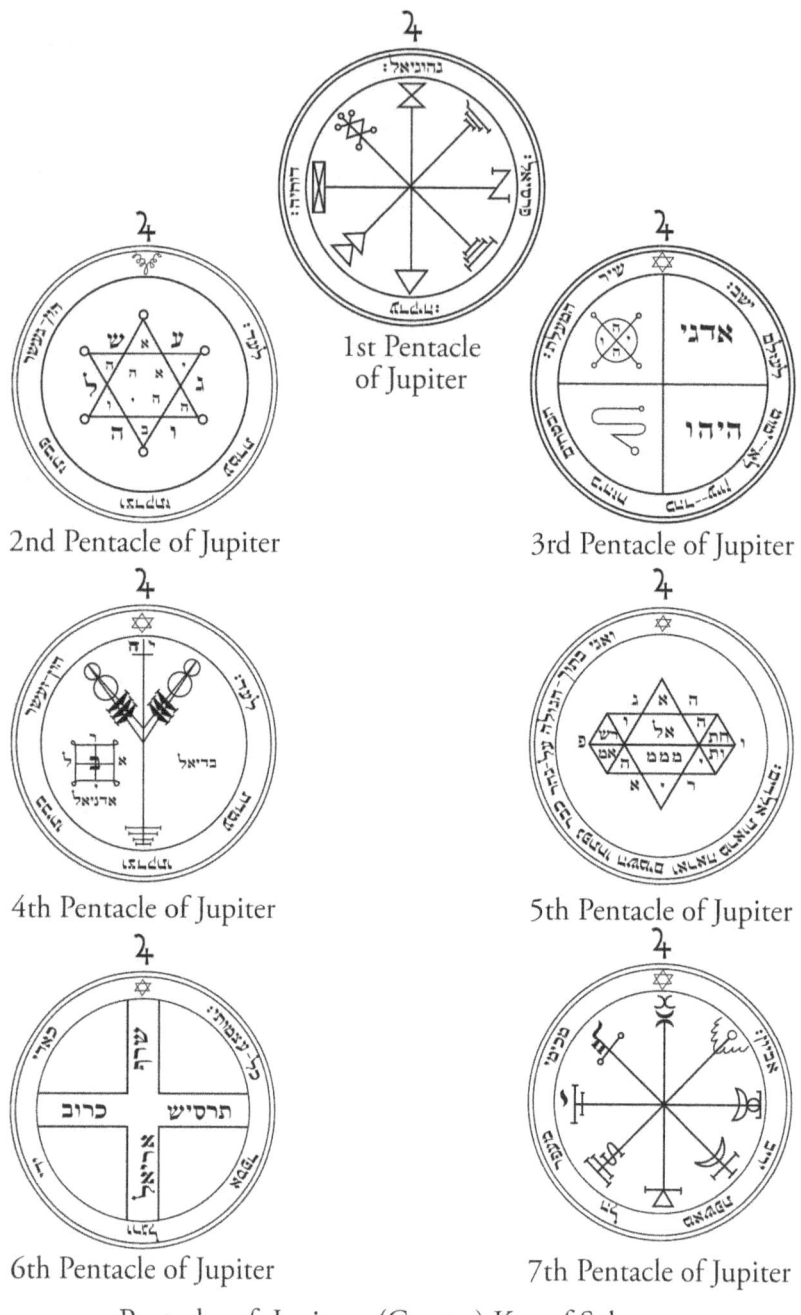

1st Pentacle of Jupiter

2nd Pentacle of Jupiter

3rd Pentacle of Jupiter

4th Pentacle of Jupiter

5th Pentacle of Jupiter

6th Pentacle of Jupiter

7th Pentacle of Jupiter

Pentacles of Jupiter - (Greater) Key of Solomon

PENTAGRAMS AND PENTACLES

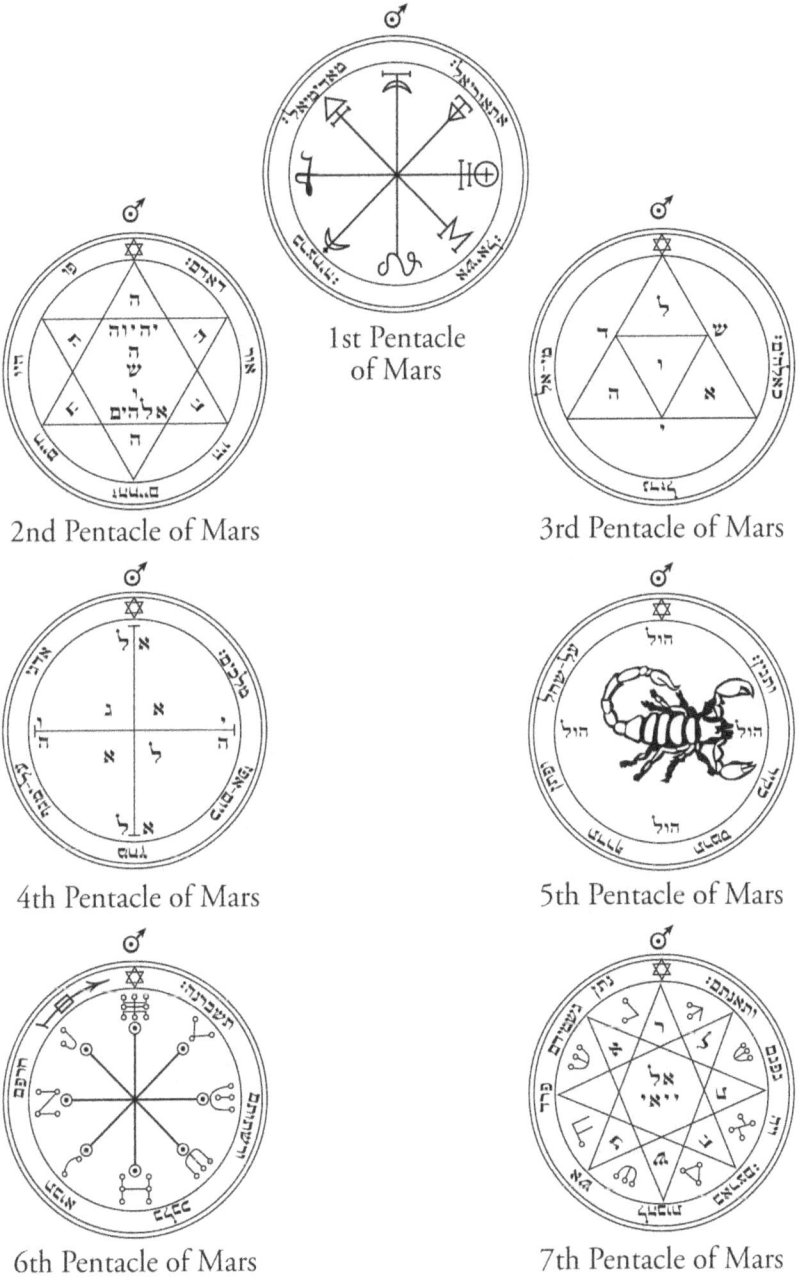

1st Pentacle of Mars

2nd Pentacle of Mars

3rd Pentacle of Mars

4th Pentacle of Mars

5th Pentacle of Mars

6th Pentacle of Mars

7th Pentacle of Mars

Pentacles of Mars - (Greater) Key of Solomon

SIGILS, SEALS AND PENTACLES

1st Pentacle of the Sun

2nd Pentacle of the Sun

3rd Pentacle of the Sun

4th Pentacle of the Sun

5th Pentacle of the Sun

6th Pentacle of the Sun

7th Pentacle of the Sun

Pentacles of the Sun - (Greater) Key of Solomon

PENTAGRAMS AND PENTACLES

1st Pentacle of Venus

2nd Pentacle of Venus

3rd Pentacle of Venus

4th Pentacle of Venus

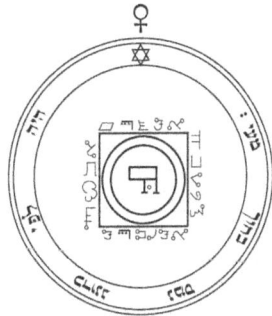

5th Pentacle of Venus

Pentacles of Venus - (Greater) Key of Solomon

1st Pentacle of Mercury

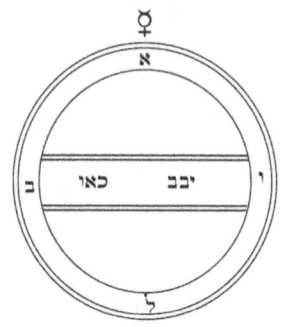
2nd Pentacle of Mercury

3rd Pentacle of Mercury

4th Pentacle of Mercury

5th Pentacle of Mercury

Pentacles of Mercury - (Greater) Key of Solomon

PENTAGRAMS AND PENTACLES

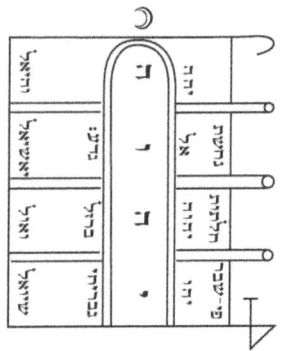
1st Pentacle of the Moon

2nd Pentacle of the Moon

3rd Pentacle of the Moon

4th Pentacle of the Moon

5th Pentacle of the Moon

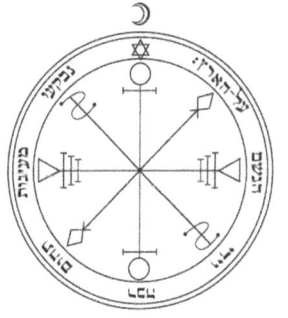
6th Pentacle of the Moon

Pentacles of the Moon - (Greater) Key of Solomon

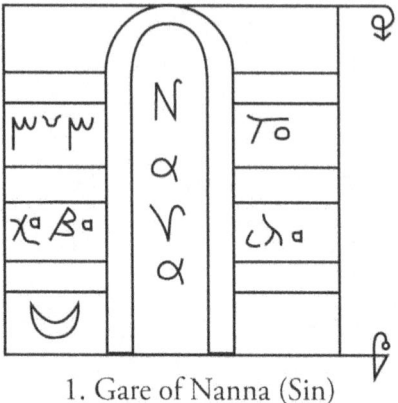

1. Gare of Nanna (Sin)

2. Gate of Nebo   3. Gate of Inana (Ishtar)

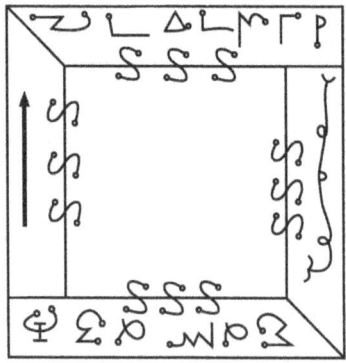

4. Gate of Shammash

Gates of the 'Simon' Necronomiccon

5. Gate of Nergal

6. Gate of Marduk

7. Gate of Nibiib

Gates of the 'Simon' Necronomiccon

Magical Furniture

The most iconic image of ceremonial magic is the figure of a magician standing in a circle featuring a pentagram, before an altar bearing a lit candle, speaking incantations to conjure a specific demonic spirit with the aid of a wand, sword and chalice. This form of ceremonial magic is called evocation, when a spirit is called before the magician and a dialogue takes place, traditionally at the point of a sword. The circle, pentagram and wand protect the magician and restrain the spirit during conjuration. They are just some of many physical objects, those items of magical furniture and implements used by the magician in the conjuration a spirit.

The magical furniture required for such operations may include a circle of consecration or a circle of conjuration that is sometimes accompanied by a triangle of evocation or constraint. An altar, situated inside the circle facing East, where the light comes from. On top of the altar is placed a cloth of the appropriate ritual colour and the necessary magical implements that may include the sword, wand, knife, incense burner, pentacle, gong or gavel, a crystal, candles and flowers. The magician will dress himself in the appropriate robes and cap, adorn himself with the appropriate pentacles, lamen and parchment talismans inscribed with magical sigils, symbols and characters.

Magic Circles
Magic Circles are part of the furniture used in ritual. They are usually drawn in chalk, salt or paint with the elemental symbols placed at the cardinal directions marked by candles around its periphery. The circle may contain a geometric shape such a pentagram, hexagram, triangle or square and they may be divided into halves or quarters.

Many types of magic circle have been used over time and the form of the circle is not always one and the same, it is according to the order of the spirits that are to be called, their places, times, days and hours.

The size of a circle can vary depending upon the purpose or philosophy. Typically, a ceremonial magic circle is nine feet in diameter, although it may be smaller or larger. Some circles are portable, divided into chambers for the ritual participants and magical instruments.

Traditionally, magicians believe that circles provided a protective barrier between themselves and what they summon. In modern times, practitioners generally cast magic circles to contain and concentrate the energy they raise in ritual.

The process of creating magic circles goes back into prehistory, made by walking in a circle, marked out using rocks and pebbles or by a length of measured cord of rope, chain, animal hide, string or cotton with the two ends left untied until the magician has entered the circle and close's it.

Circles can also be drawn into soft ground using a finger, stick or pointed weapon such as a wand or sword but is traditionally drawn with a magic spear, a practice which may go back as far as Neolithic hunting rituals. Circles are also visualized, as many magicians claim there is no need to use a circle unless summoning very powerful spirits. In Greco-Egyptian papyri, the circle is scarcely mentioned with the magician relying on protection from amulets worn on his person.

Some circles require the magician to stand outside the circle, some to stand inside it, others have gates to allow entry into the inner circle. Sometimes the energy being summoned appears within the circle, other times it appears in a separately drawn triangle. But most importantly, the specific design is the nature of the mystical words and symbols drawn inside it.

The oldest written circles are Mesopotamian magic bowls dating from the 4th and 6th centuries BCE. They have many of the characteristics that medieval and renaissance sorcerers used, including spirals of text. The bowls also employ the abbreviated names of gods and spirits, some also have quartered circles.

The earliest form of modern circles first appeared in the Byzantine Empire in the early years of Christianity. The English occultist Robert Marlowe describes magic circles during Elizabethan times as containing the name Jehovah spelt forwards and backwards and the abbreviated names of saints, the signs and symbols of the elements, the planets and the zodiac by which the spirits are enforced to rise. Written on parchment or cloth they were generally talismanic.

In many grimoires, magicians are urged to reinforce the circle by writing various names of power along its circumference. These names are mostly culled from the various forms of the Tetragrammaton. They can be written on the ground or on cards and placed strategically around inner edge of the circle. Three favourite names are El Shaddai El Chai, Tetragrammaton and Ararita.

Circle and Triangle

In ceremonial magic, a circle of conjuration is a magic circle drawn to protect the magician from malevolent spirits, it is often accompanied by a triangle of evocation or constraint, placed at an eastern point outside the circle.

In the circle and triangle combination, the center circle is the circle of conjuration, drawn to protect the magician from malevolent spirits and inscribed with the sigil or seal of the spirit to be invoked. The outer ring has words of power inscribed around its circumference.

Most circles of conjuration generally contain the name of God, both Christian and Jewish, alongside the names of angels, fragments of liturgy, written in Hebrew, Greek, Latin, English or other magical languages and their scripts. When the circle has been constructed, lamps or candles are placed at each quarter point of the circle that are considered as 'cardinal', north, south, east, west, which are related to the four Archangels, Michael, Gabriel, Raphael, Uriel, or to the four elements, air, fire, water, earth, and are associated with the four names of God. Other ceremonial traditions have candles placed between the quarters, i.e., northwest, northeast, southwest, southeast.

There are also common ceremonial colour attributions for the quarter candles, yellow for air in the east, red for fire in the south, blue for water in the west and green for earth in the north. This can vary depending on geographical location and individual philosophy.

The magic triangle known as the triangle of evocation or constraint is mainly a diagram for putting the magician into contact with the energy, power or being to be employed. Its main purpose is to confine any spirit that has been conjured to visible appearance

The triangle is circumscribed with various words of power, containing an inner, blackened circle, sometimes this central circle is replaced with a black scrying mirror. In some cases, the triangle is created as a physical object.

Solomonic Circle and Triangle
The magic of Solomon has used many circle designs in its history. One of the oldest comes from the 14th century Greek grimoire, the Magical Treatise of Solomon. The 16th century grimoire, the Heptameron features a magic circle attributed to Solomon. The Key of Solomon features a circle of consecration as well as a circle of conjuration and the Lesser Key of Solomon has several variants of the same circle of conjuration, the most famous includes a drawing of a coiled serpent containing divine names.

In the Ars Goetia of the Lesser Key of Solomon, the circle of conjuration is nine feet across, the space between the inner and outer circles is coloured yellow and contains divine names, beginning at EHYEH and ending at LEVANAH, written around it in Hebrew, in a spiral arrangement within the double circle (the coiled serpent is only shown in one private codex). The small Maltese crosses are placed to mark the conclusion of each separate set of Hebrew names. These names are those of the deity, angels and archangels allotted by the cabalists to each of the nine Sephiroth or Divine Emanations.

The square in the center of the circle, where the word "master" is written, is filled in with red. All names and letters are in black. In the Hexagrams, the outer triangles where the letters a, d, o, n, a, i, appear are filled in with bright yellow and the centers, where the T-shaped crosses are, blue or green. In the Pentagrams outside the circle, the outer triangles where "Te, tra, gram, ma, ton," is written are filled in bright yellow, and the centers with the T crosses written therein are red. It is to be remembered that Hebrew is always written from right to left, not left to right like European languages.

Solomon commanded the evil spirits into a magical triangle, placed in the quarter to where the spirit belongs. The triangle is three feet across and the base of the triangle is to be placed nearest the circle, at a distance of two feet from the circle. The apex pointing to the direction of the quarter of the spirit. The triangle is outlined in black, the name of Michael is black on white, the three names outside the triangle are written in red, and the center circle filled entirely in dark green.

Enochian Ceremonial Circle

The Enochian ceremonial circle is nine feet wide at the inner circle and ten feet at the outer circle. Written in-between the inner and outer circle are the Enochian names of the elements. The names of the elements relate to the position of four triangles placed between the cardinal points to represent the 'elemental' Watchtowers, the spiritual guardians of the cardinal points. When conducting magical operations on the Watchtowers, sit or stand in the circle whose colour can vary according to operations, generally green is appropriate for most operations. However, colour should correspond with the magical operation in which it is used. South – fire/red/BITOM, North – earth/black/NANTA, West – water/blue/HKOMA, East – air/yellow/EYARRD.

Post-Modern Circles

In the second half of the 20th century, the advent of neopaganism in Europe and North America led to a re-imagining of the Witch's or Wiccan circle. Called a Pentacle or Pentan, it is nine feet in diameter and at its center it usually contains a pentagram or more rarely a triquetra interlocked with a circle. The five cardinal points of the pentagram are represented by their elemental symbols or names written in runic script, in their associated colour. In the 1960s, the New Age Counter Culture produced its own magic circles relating to the magic of the Age of Aquarius.

The Book of Calling from the 'Simon' Necronomicon, shows designs called Mandal's of Calling that are drawn inside a circle. In some rituals, the Seals of the Gates are placed around the Mandal's circumference, representing the cardinal directions or watchtowers.

In the early 21st century, Barry William Hale created the Circle of Beelzebub, a circle of evocation. Hale used Austin Osman Spare's 'sigilisation' technique, in which the spirit's signature is represented by a sigil created from the binding of the individual letters of the spirit's name.

Hale utilizes Spare's technique to form the central sigil of Beelzebub and create a sigillic recension of the corresponding incantation within the circular constraints of the composition. The Circle of Beelzebub was an appendant artwork to Legion 49.

Altars and Tables of Practice

Other important item of magical furniture are the altar and tables of practice. In ritual magic, an altar is situated inside the circle and faces East. On top of the altar is placed a cloth of the appropriate ritual colour and the necessary magical implements.

An altar serves as a sacred space for performing spiritual rituals and spell work. It is often the focus of religious ceremony and is normally the center of ritual. In prehistory, altars were mere piles of stone. The Egyptians used altars made of massive blocks of baked clay. The Romans used indoor altars to celebrate the spirits of the house and family. For Christians, the altar assumes a central role in celebrations and is often decorated majestically.

Tables of Practice are used to evoke specific groups of angels, In the Ars Pauline of the Lesser Key of Solomon, there is a Table of Practice for the summoning of the 24 angels of the hours of the day and night. Their seals are to be placed upon the corresponding planetary elemental character, one of the seven Seals of the Elements that that are the central feature of the Table. They are based on the characters of the seven planets from the magical calendar. When the seal is in the correct place, the hand is to be laid upon it and the conjuration is spoken.

In Enochian magic, the Holy Table of Practice holds the Seal of Ameth. It is a symbolic representation of the Enochian universe. Dee and Kelly were first given instructions for creating the Holy Table and introduced to the Seal of Ameth before any of the other Enochian material. The Holy Table is made of beeswax and engraved with a hexagram and surrounded by a boarder of Enochian letters and in the center, a ritual table or cell is engraved with individual Enochian letters.

The Angels then presented them with the seven Ensigns of Creation, that act as talismans when they are painted directly on to the Table of Practice or engraved on tablets of purified Tin and placed around the Table in a clockwise direction. They are to be used as a means of establishing 'consultations' between the magician and the heptarchic powers.

The Seal of Ameth, also made of beeswax is engraved with various lineal figures, letters and numbers. The Table of Practice requires five Seals of Ameth for its operations, four small ones are placed under the feet of the Holy Table. The fifth and larger one is about nine inches wide and covered in a red cloth, placed in the center of the table and is used to support the 'shew stone' or 'speculum', a 'scrying' device such as a crystal or obsidian mirror.

The Great Table of the Zonei appears in the hoax version of the Necronomicon attributed to the Enochian Magician Dr. John Dee. A copy of which is said to be kept in the library of Philadelphia University. The Great Table operates along the same lines of other tables, for the Calling of the Sumerian deities corresponding to the seven planets.

SIGILS, SEALS AND PENTACLES

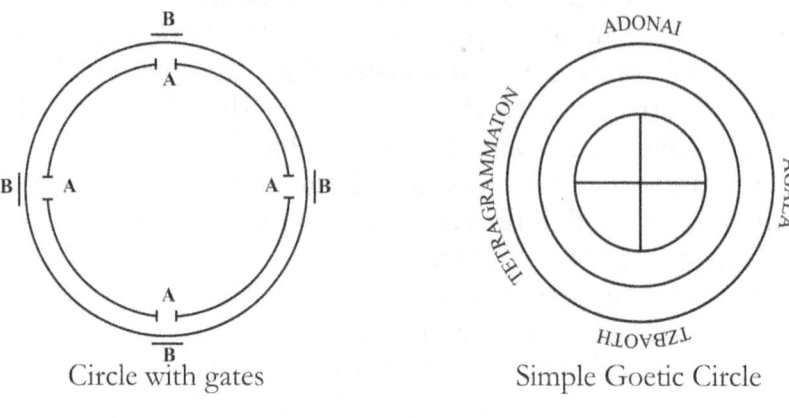

Circle with gates   Simple Goetic Circle

Circle for All Conjurations

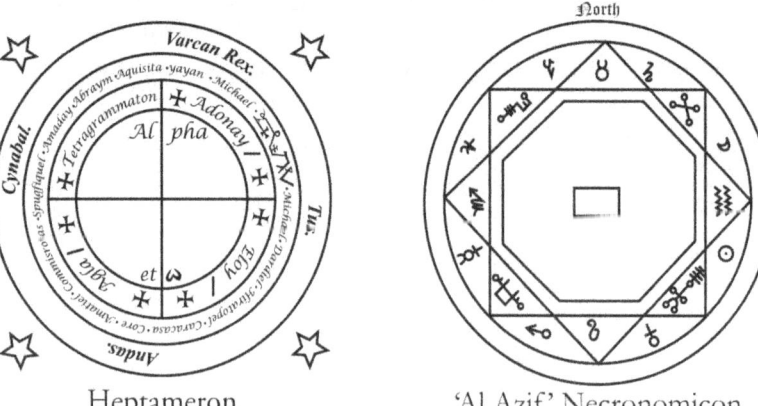

Heptameron   'Al Azif' Necronomicon

Circles of Conjuration

MAGICAL FURNITURE

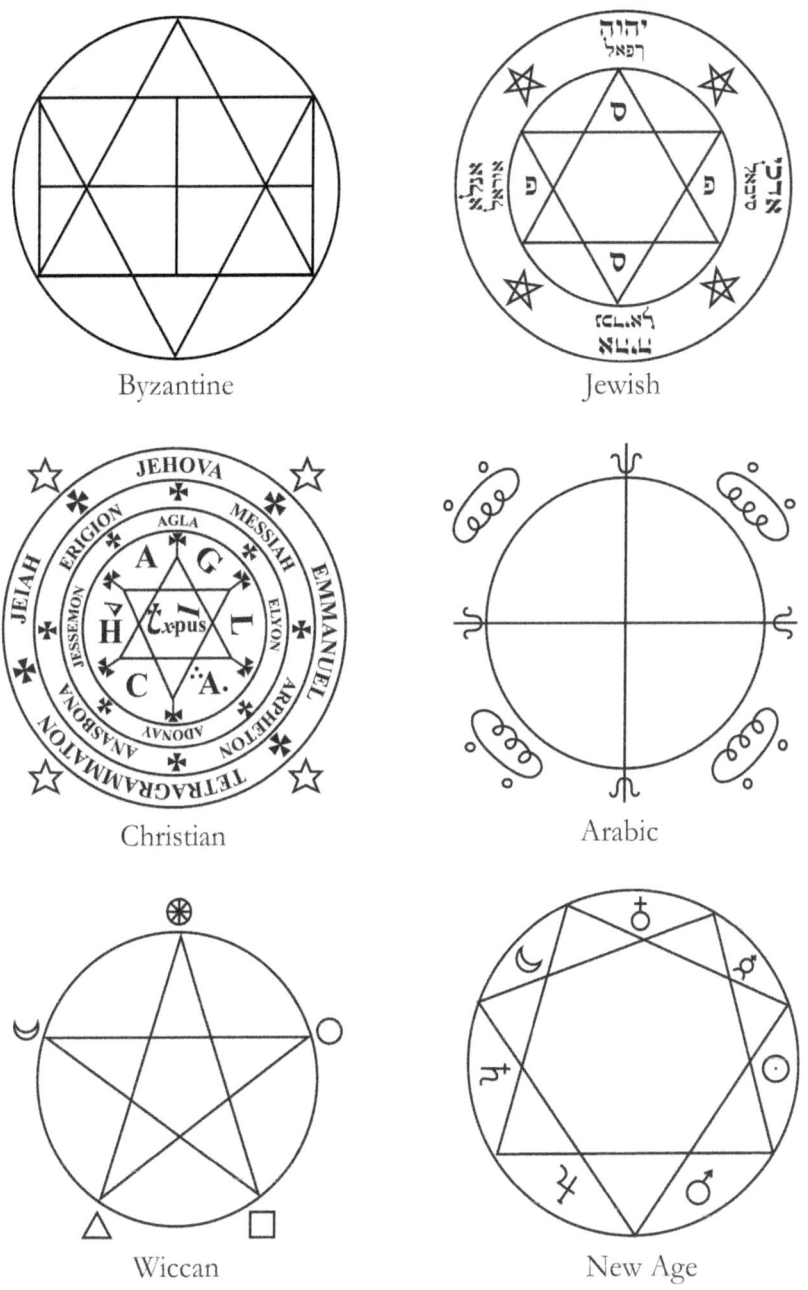

Byzantine — Jewish — Christian — Arabic — Wiccan — New Age

Circles of Conjuration

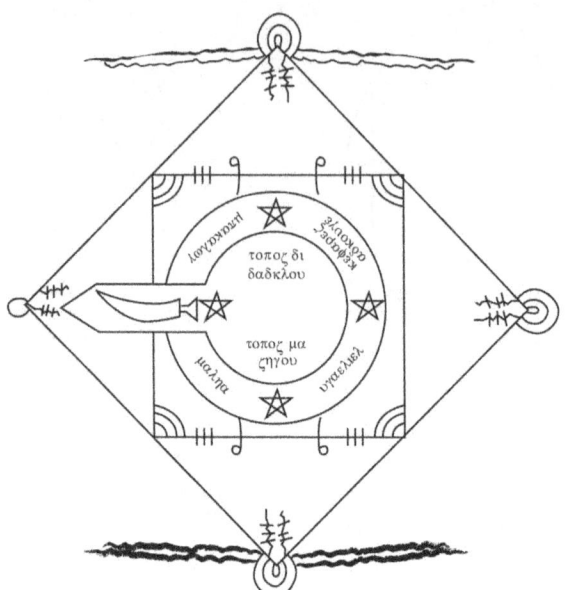

14th / 15th c. Greek Manuscript

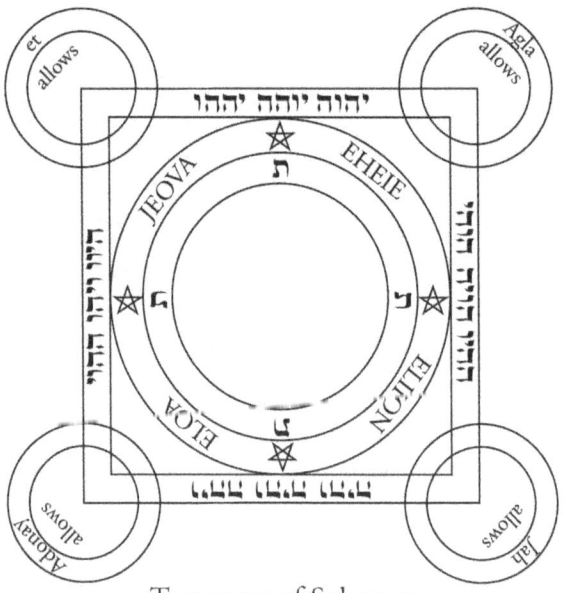

Testament of Solomon

Circles of Solomon

MAGICAL FURNITURE

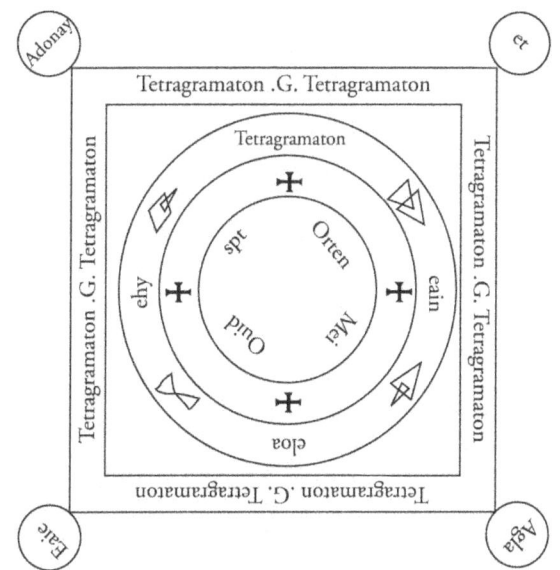

Solomon's Circle - Heptameron

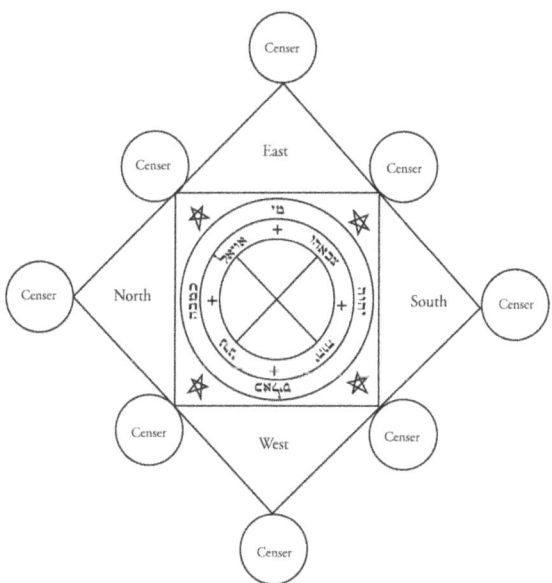

(Greater) Key of Solomon
Circles of Solomon

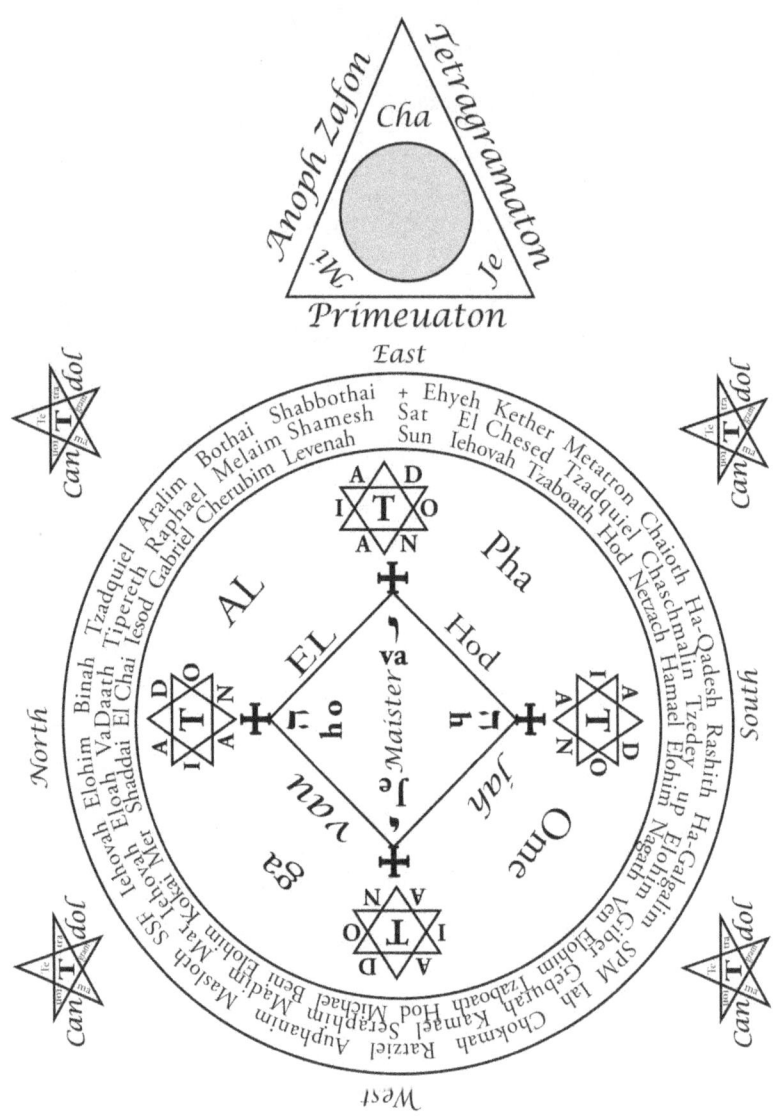

Circle and Triangle of Solomon
Lesser Keys of Solomon

MAGICAL FURNITURE

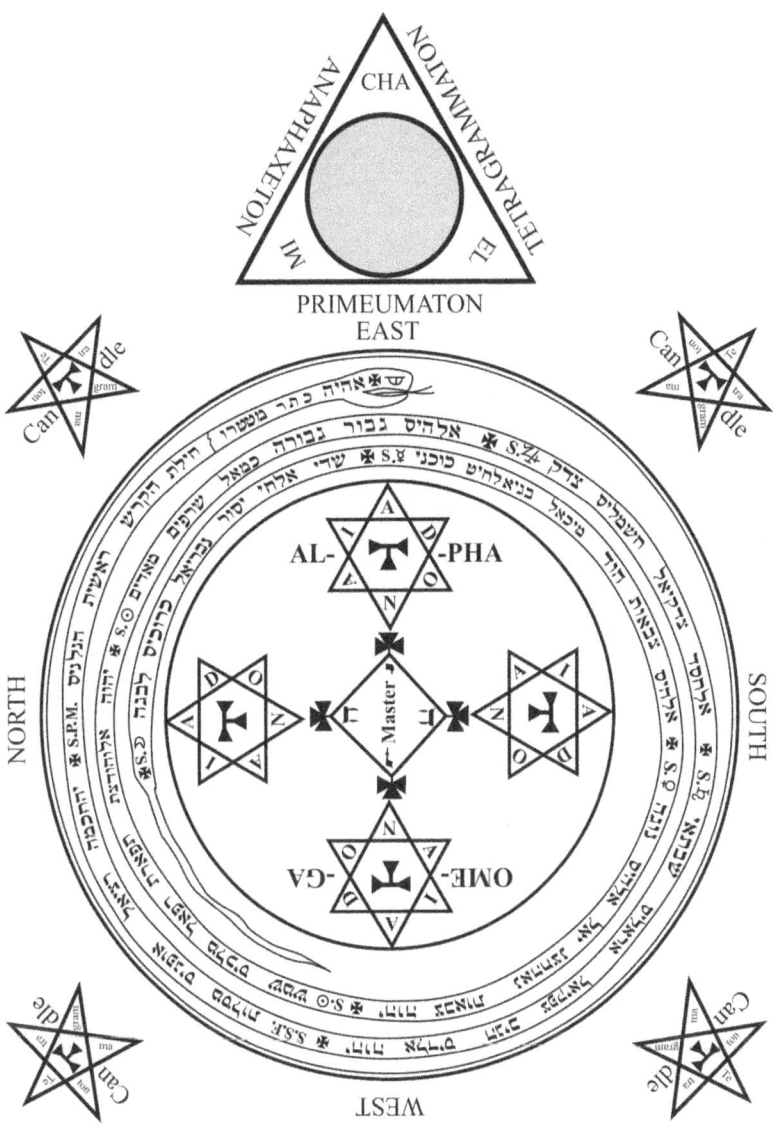

Circle and Triangle of Solomon
Book of Goetia of Solomon the King - S L Mathers

Enochian Circle of Evocation

Wiccan Pentans

MAGICAL FURNITURE

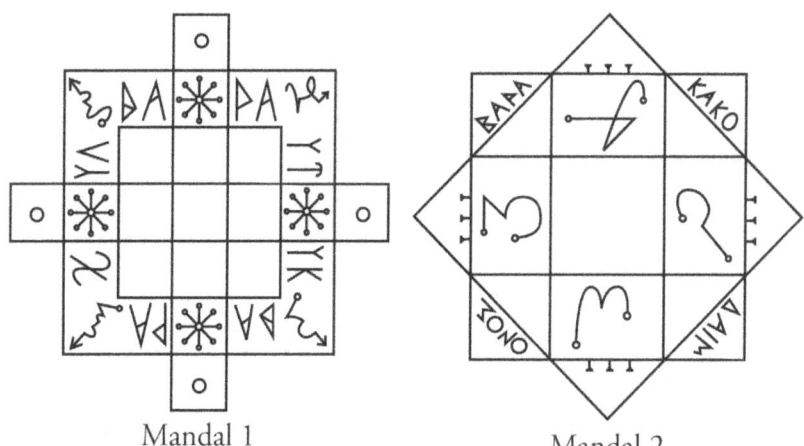

Mandal 1 Mandal 2
Mandal's of Calling - 'Simon' Necronomicon

Circle of Beelzebub - Legion 49 / Barry William Hale

SIGILS, SEALS AND PENTACLES

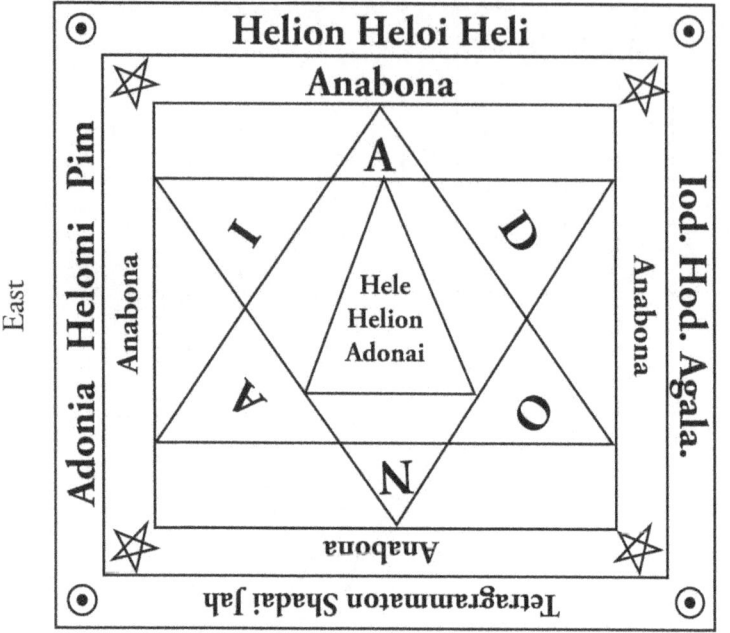

Almadel (portable alter) Lesser Keys of Solomon - Ars Almadel

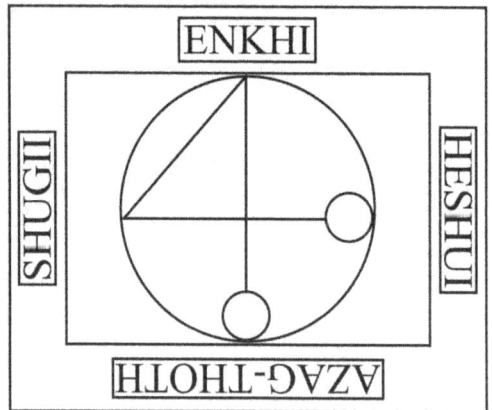

Table or Alter of Invocation
Necronomicon - Dr John Dee

MAGICAL FURNITURE

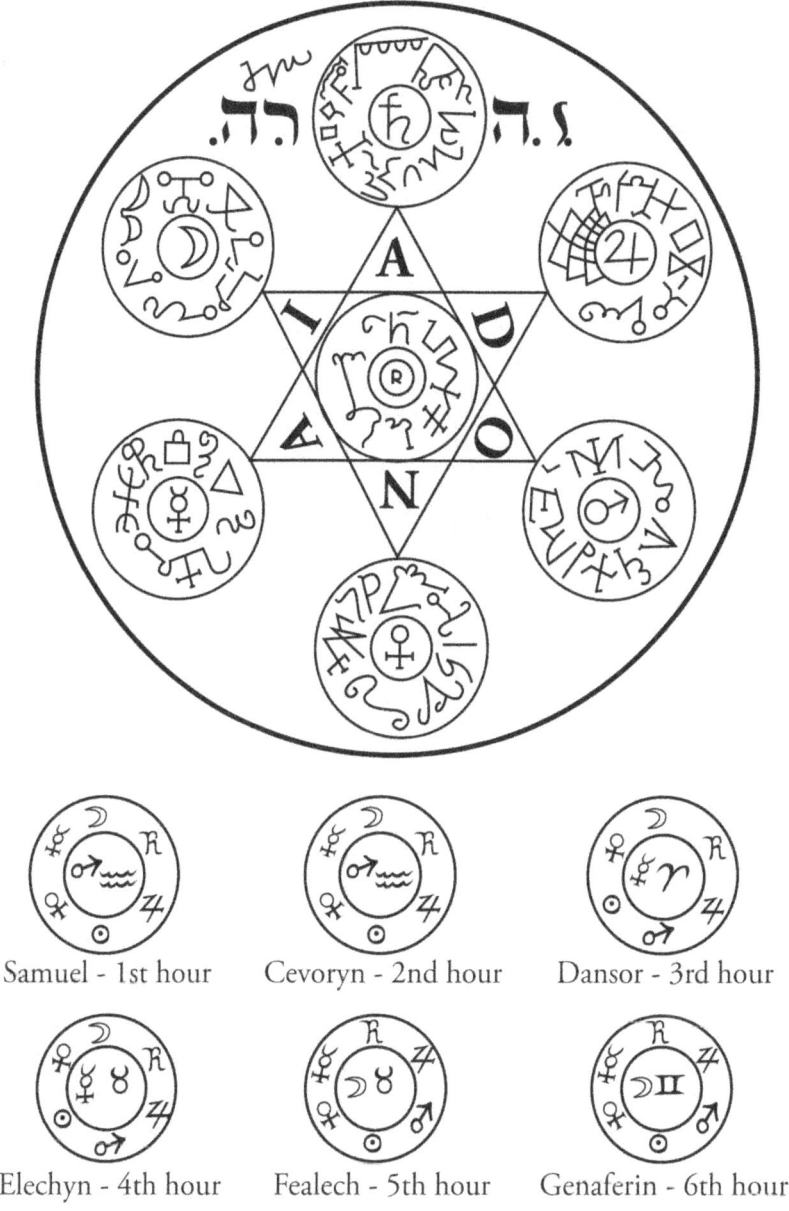

Samuel - 1st hour   Cevoryn - 2nd hour   Dansor - 3rd hour

Elechyn - 4th hour   Fealech - 5th hour   Genaferin - 6th hour

Table of Practise and some of the
Seals of the Angels of the Hours of the Day and Night
Lesser Key of Solomon - Ars Pauline

SIGILS, SEALS AND PENTACLES

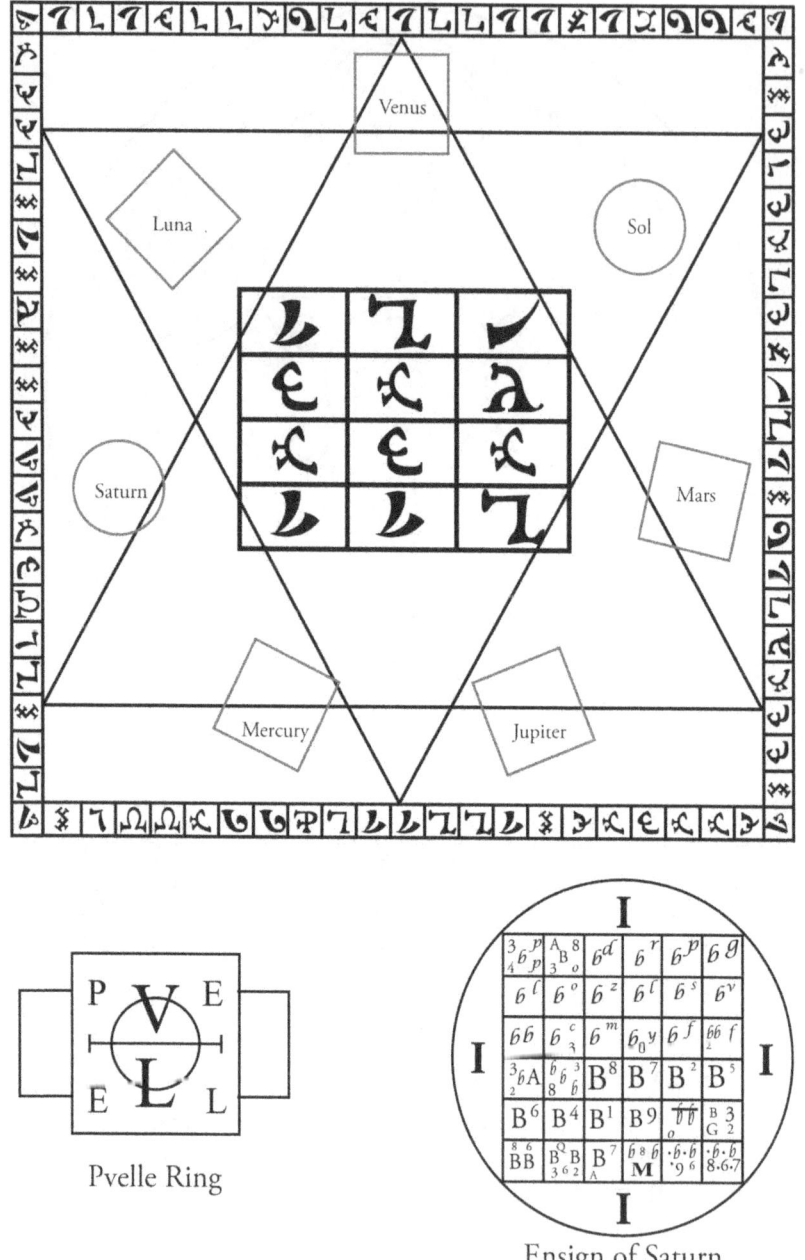

Pvelle Ring

Ensign of Saturn

Holy Table of Practice and the Ensigns of Creation - Dr John Dee

MAGICAL FURNITURE

Ensign of Jupiter

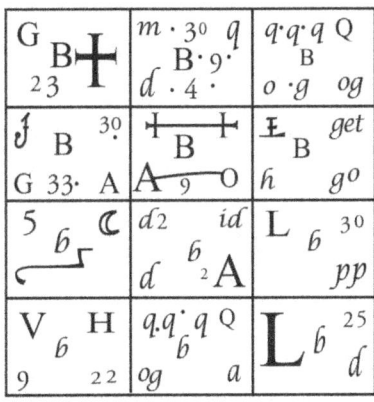

Emsign of Mars

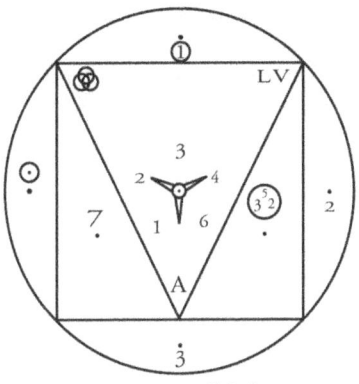

Ensign of Sol

Ensign of Venus

Ensign of Mercury

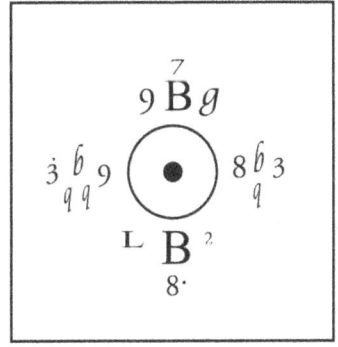

Ensign of Luna

SIGILS, SEALS AND PENTACLES

Great Table of the Zonei

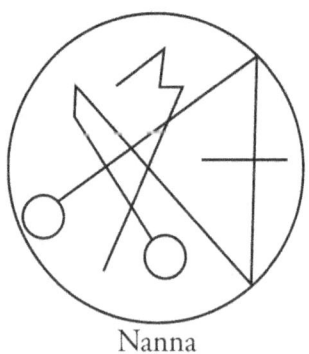

Nanna

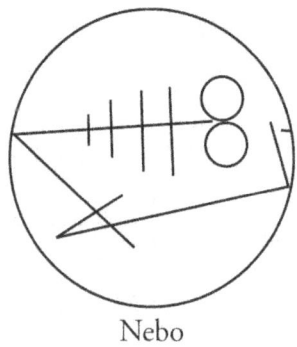

Nebo

MAGICAL FURNITURE

Inana

Shammash

Nergal

Marduk

Ninib

Yoggoth

Great Table and Seals of the Zonei
Necronomicon - Dr. John Dee

Magical Implements

Like most magical furniture, most magical implements are physical objects, consecrated for a specific ritual and adorned with sigils and characters. There are many magic implements employed by the magician for different operations that can be found mainly on the altar top or worn about the body.

In Wiccan ritual, magical tools include a ritual sword or knife called an Athame. A wand made of wood, metal or stone that can be set with gemstones or crystals. A Boline, a knife with a curved blade. A censor and incense, a scourge, a singlum (girdle/belt), a Besom or broom, cauldron, spear (Odin) and a smudge stick. The chalice or cup is not considered to be a tool, instead it is a symbol of the Goddess, especially the womb.

The tools required by the Key of Solomon include the wand, chalice, scepter, knife, sword, sickle, poniard, dagger, short lance, staff and other objects like candles, incense burner, herb sprinklers and virgin parchment.

They differ slightly from the tools employed in the goetic practice of the Lesser Key of Solomon. The magic implements listed include a girdle of lion's skin, three inches broad and inscribed with the same names as the outermost part of the circle, anointing oil, a chaffing dish and charcoal for perfumes and incense.

Elemental Weapons

Magic implements are often described as weapons. Magical weapons are real or vividly imagined props used as physical devices to help focus the mind during the magical operations.

The title 'weapons' goes back to a time in the ancient world, when one of the primary duties of the magician was to preform apotropaic magic that drives away evil, some of the earliest wands were just bundles of sticks or branches. Apotropaic wands used by the Egyptians were made out of ivory, curved like throwing sticks, and carved with the images of protective deities. Eventually, different types of wand and other implements were developed for different purposes.

These weapons are divided into categories and attributed with a variety of combat powers, to almost always improve attacks. Armour, shields and weapons give protection to the wearer, wands are short sticks imbued with the power to cast a specific spell with each use depleting its charge, a rod is a scepter like item whose charge depletes with use, or a staff whose charge depletes with use.

However, describing these implements as weapons of battle gives an inaccurate portrayal of how these weapons work. Rather than think of them as weapons of battle to battle spirits, they should be thought of as talismanic badges of authority, used to open portals between different spiritual realms and energies, consecrated passkeys to the unseen realms.

Collectively known as the 'elemental weapons', the four magical implements used by the Golden Dawn in Enochian rites are the Fire Wand, Water Cup, Air Dagger and Earth Pentacle. All the elemental weapons are inscribed with divine names and sigils and painted in the flashing colours that relate to their respective elements.

Those used by the Golden Dawn have specific functions. The Earth Pentacle is a flat disc that serves as a container for magical forces, when fully charged it is a powerful source of energy and sustenance, symbolizing food and nourishment, the magician's body as a form of crystalized karma. It protects the magician from the evil forces in the quadrant of earth.

The Water Cup is a passive weapon representing the magicians understanding of magic. It is feminine and can be used to counter attacks from the forces of the masculine currents. It will protect the magician from the evil forces in the quadrant of water.

The Air sword and the Air dagger will protect against the evil forces of the quadrant of air. Both weapons are used to counter illusion. The Air Sword symbolizes logic and reason. It cuts and dissects like the mind, when focused on a complex idea. Its nature is division and separation. It is attributed to Geburah and Mars and can be aptly be described as a spiritual weapon. They state that the sword should be used in all cases where great force and strength are needed, but especially for banishing and defense against evil forces. The Dagger pierces like the penetrating power of thought against illusion, cutting through the illusion of the mind

The Fire Wand symbolizes the Will. It is the principle weapon of The Magus and can be used for both invocation and evocation. It is the chief weapon used to combat all types of energy and will protect the magician from the evil forces of the quadrant of fire.

Other weapons used are the 'Pvelle' ring and the rod 'El'. The Ring symbolizes protection. The design for the ring was revealed to Dee by the Archangel Michael in a dream. It is made of gold and is magically designed to protect the wearer from all manner of evil influences. According to Dee "wherewith all miracles and divine works and wonders were wrought by Solomon". The rod is painted in three sections, the ends being black, the middle being red.

Aleister Crowley listed his required magic implements as a circle inscribed with the name of God, an altar and a phial of oil, a wand, a cup, sword and a pentacle. Also, a scourge, dagger and chain, an oil lamp, a book of conjurations, a bell and a crown, a robe and a lamen.

Part of the magicians armour is the 'lamen' or 'plate', a magical pendant or breastplate worn around the neck so that it hangs upon the breast over the heart. Its uses vary but most commonly, the term refers to a symbol of authority and a focus of magical energies. The magician may wear a lamen as a representation of his personal relationship to his Godhead or the universal forces of balance and enlightenment. It expresses the character and power of the wearer. Aleister Crowley described the lamen as 'a sort of coat of arms'. He and others have proposed that the magical lamen might be a modern adaptation of the priestly breastplate of the ancient Hebrews.

Within a group ceremony, lamen are frequently worn as symbols of particular offices or roles within the ritual work. Many magic orders also us a particular lamen design to show membership and align energies of individual members with the group dynamic. Lamen may also be used to evoke certain spirits in Solomonic magic and specialized lamen are used by various magic orders in one or more ways.

Callings of the Necronomicon

The 'Simon' Necronomicon is a post-modern collection of magic rituals and conjurations, in which many incantations and seals are described. The many magical seals pertain to particular gods and demons, used when invoking or summoning the entity with which it is associated. There are also specific instructions on how to inscribe the seals and amulets. It is made up of many books including the Book of Calling, giving information on the magical implements to be used in evocation.

In its Ceremonies of Calling, any spirit may be summoned and detained. The Place of Calling should be in a secluded place far from the thoughts of man, a mountain top, a desert or by the sea. A Mandal of Calling shall be drawn within a circle on the ground in lime, barley or white flour, or dug in the ground with the Dagger of Inanna of Calling. Or embroidered in the most precious silk or expensive cloth and the colours shall be black and white and no other.

The Frontlet and Standards of Calling shall be of fine cloth and in the colours of black and white. And the Crown of Calling shall bear the eight-rayed star of the Elder Gods and may be made of beaten copper, set in with precious stones. And thou shalt bear a Rod of Lapis lazuli, the five-rayed star about thy neck, the Frontlet of Calling, the Girdle, the Amulet of UR about thine arm, and a pure and unspotted Robe.

The Crown of Anu is the Frontpeice of Calling and is used in many rituals. In the Exorcism of the Crown of Anu, the priest shall put on the spotless white crown of Anu with the eight rayed seal with the Tablet of Calling on his breast and the copper dagger of Inanna in his right hand aloft.

In the Conjuration of The Watcher, the Four Gates of the cardinal directions are invoked, being the Four Watchtowers that stand about the circumference of the Mandal of Calling.

MAGICAL IMPLEMENTS

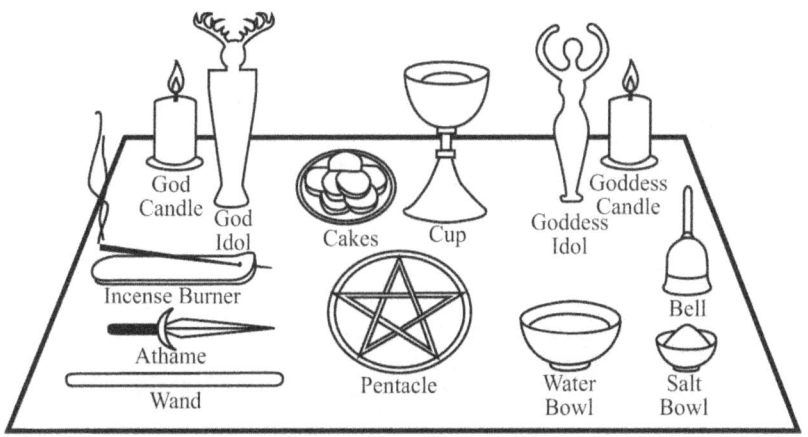

Placement of Ritual Tools on the Witch's Altar

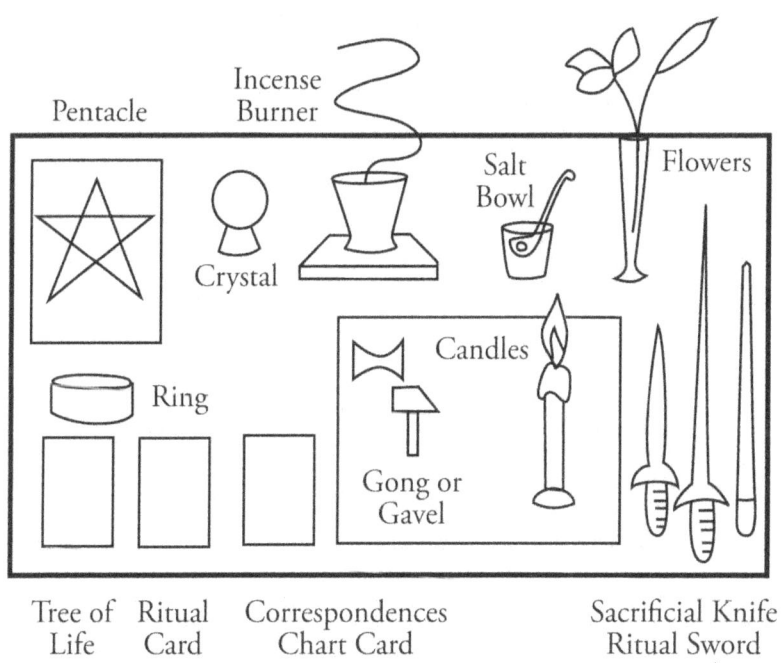

Placement of Ritual Tools on the Ceremonial Altar

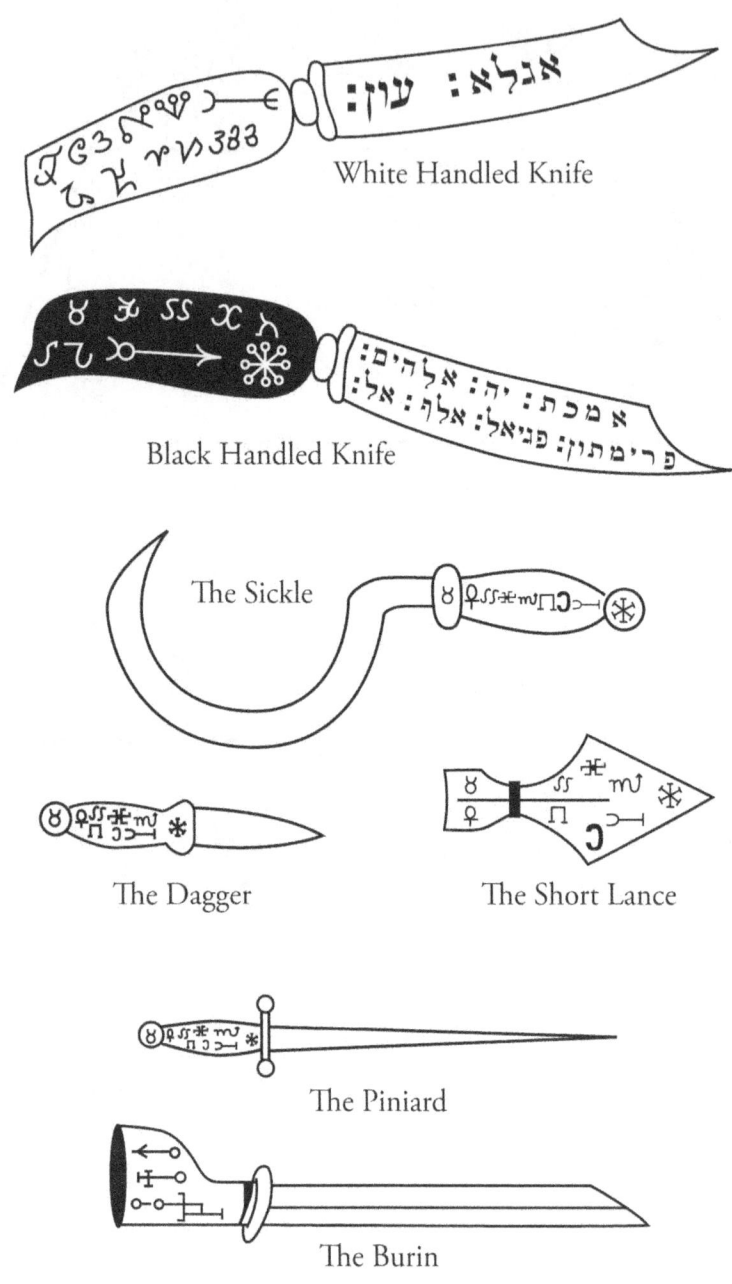

Magic Weapons - (Greater) Key of Solomon

MAGICAL IMPLEMENTS

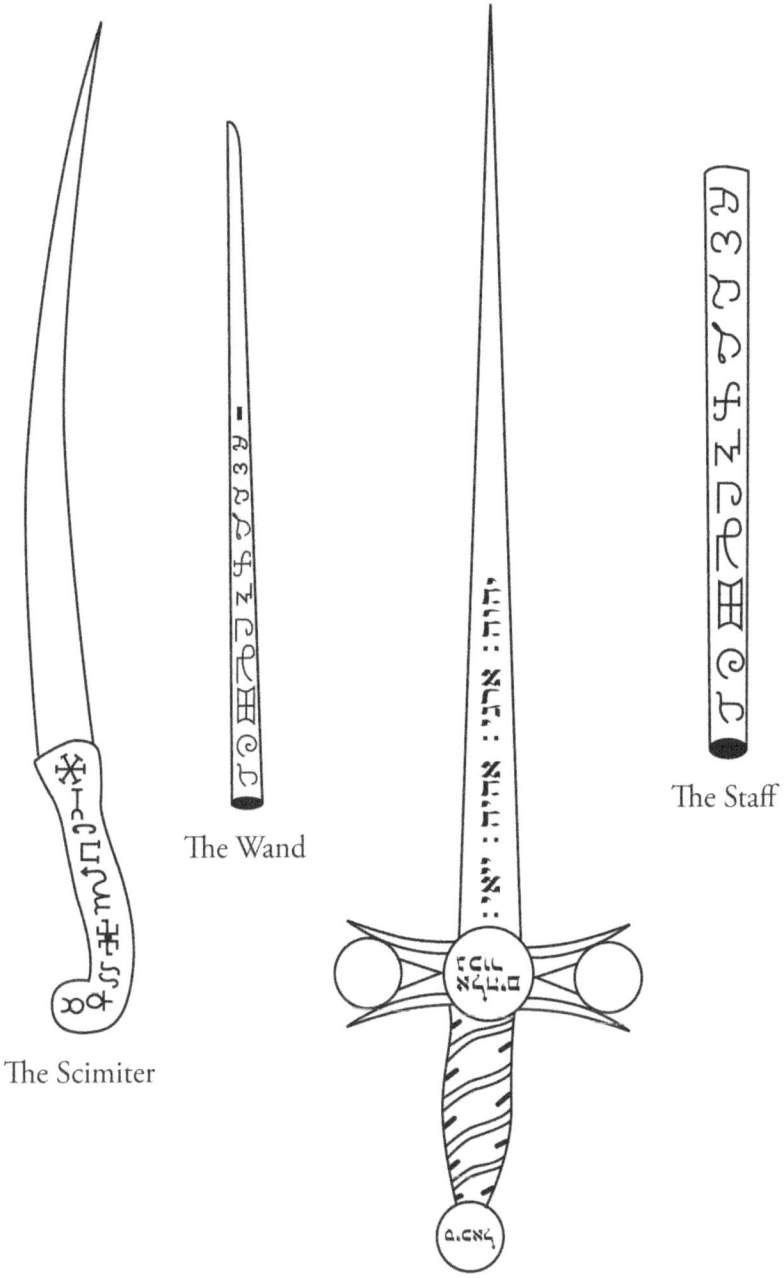

The Scimiter

The Wand

The Magical Sword

The Staff

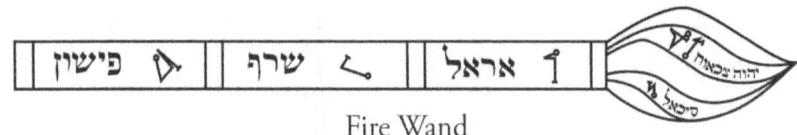

Fire Wand

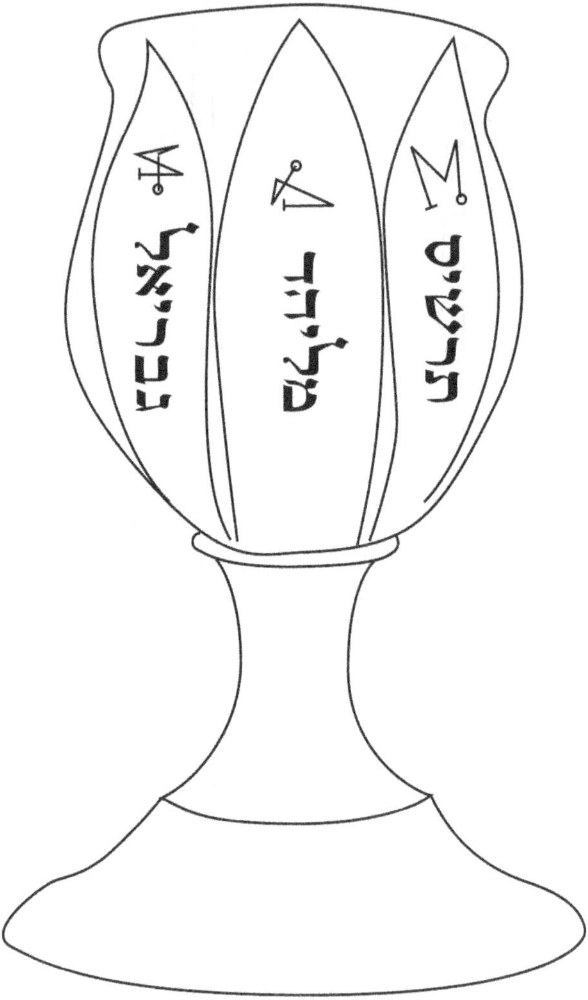

Water Chalice

Elementtal Weapons - Golden Dawn Enocxhian Magic

MAGICAL IMPLEMENTS

Air Dagger

Earth Pentacle

Elementtal Weapons - Golden Dawn Enocxhian Magic

Lamin / Lamen
Lesser Keys of Solomon - Ars Paulina

MAGICAL IMPLEMENTS

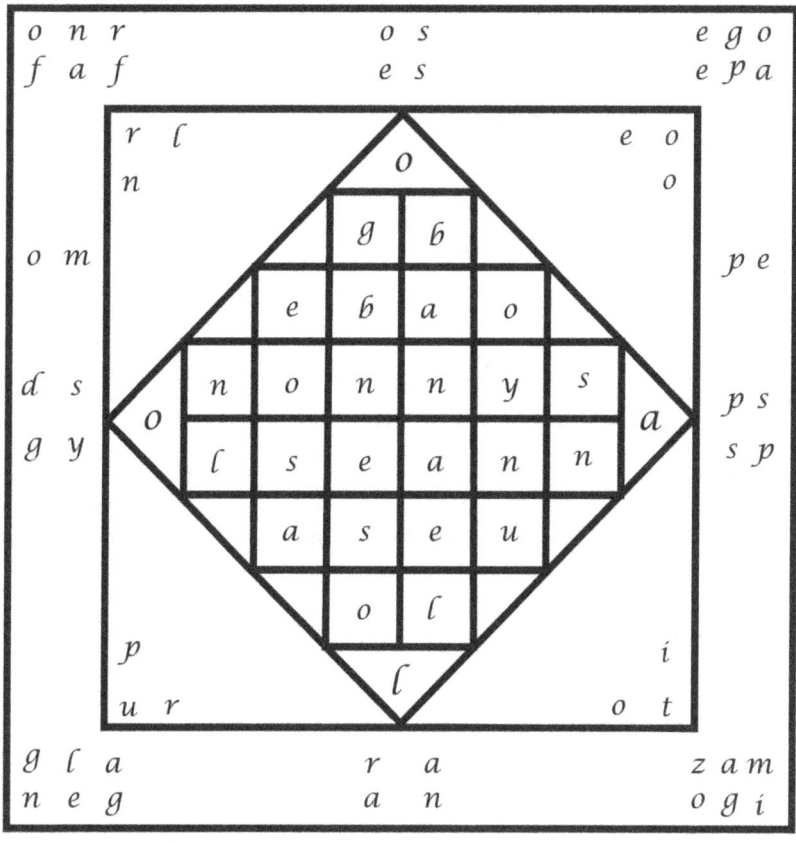

Lamin / Lamen
Libra Hrptarchia Mystica - Dr John Dee

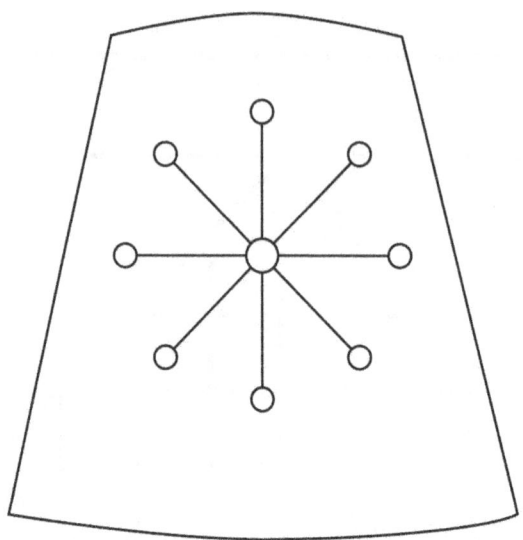

Anu's Crown of Calling

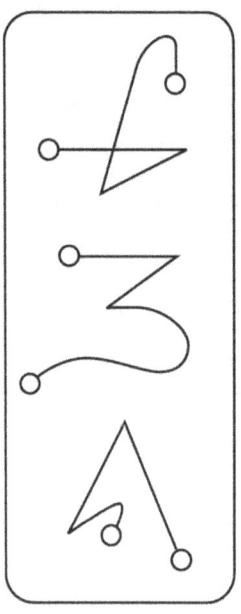

Frontlet of Calling

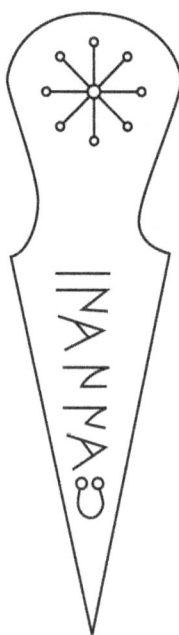

Inanna's Dagger of Calling

MAGICAL IMPLEMENTS

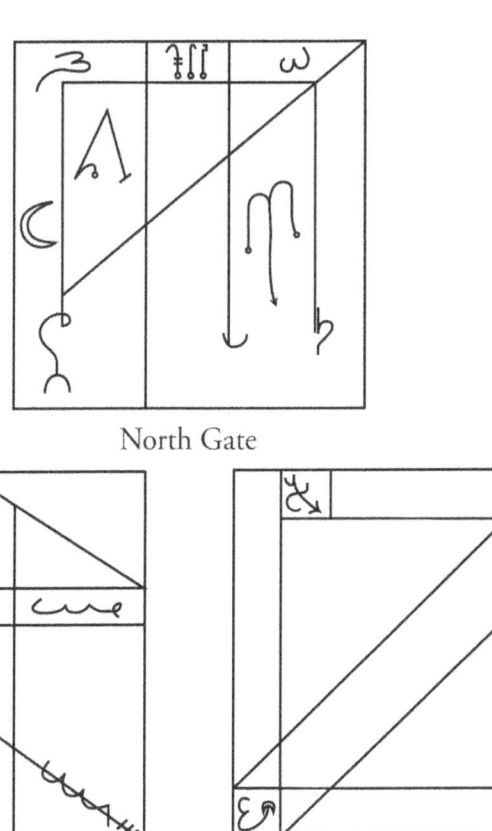

North Gate

West Gate

East Gate

South Gate

Implements of Calling / Book of Calling - "Simon" Necronomicon

Symbols and Scripts

Many of the occult designs employed in the practice of ceremonial magic have magic symbols, characters and scripts inscribed on them. Among the most common are planetary and astrological symbols, the mystical glyphs referred to as magical characters and those occult scripts considered to be endowed with great magical power due to their origin or antiquity.

Both astrology and astronomy use ancient symbols to depict planets, stars and constellations. The seven planets and the twelve signs of the zodiac are each distinguished by a special symbol. Those symbols have become increasingly popular in modern times, worn around the neck as symbols good luck or self-assertion.

The Chaldeans and Babylonians were the first people to make a meticulous study of astrology. In Babylon, there were five visible planets, Mercury, Venus, Mars, Jupiter and Saturn with the Sun and Moon being luminaries. Together they form the seven planets of ancient times. Each planet was believed to rule over a metal, colour, stones, herbs, flowers, trees, fruit, perfumes and animals.

The practice spread to Egypt, to Greece and eventually Rome. During the Middle Ages, it was a scholarly subject it which it was necessary to know Latin, Geek and Hebrew and sometimes Arabic, as well as complicated mathematical computations in order to be an astrologer.

Planetary and Astrological Symbols

Planetary symbols are based on their association with a particular metal and are not as well-known as those of the zodiac. Planetary characters are sets of divine signs containing both the good and the bad influences of the planets.

Astrological signs are graphic forms of the occult interpretations of the constellations of the Zodiac. Each of the twelve astrological signs is ruled by a planet. The exceptions are Taurus and Libra who share Venus, and Virgo and Gemini who share Mercury.

Magic Scripts

Seals and pentacles often contain the names of God and angels, their names are often written in a magic script to hide them from the uninitiated. An enormous number of magic scripts have been recorded in the western occult tradition, very many of them being of a somewhat dubious value, but a few of them used in occult literature or in various art forms have an occult heritage. Some of these scripts are reinterpreted versions of genuine historical alphabets that have been collated from occult texts and a great many more are derived from cabalistic sources.

The most magical of these scripts were documented by Henrich Cornelius Agrippa in his Books of Occult Philosophy and the same scripts can be seen in a Table of the Mystical Alphabets found in the Key of Solomon. They were more often than not based on Judeo-Greek cabalistic principles, acting as codes and ciphers for hiding the esoteric knowledge or communicating with angels.

During the Middle Ages, it became popular to write the names of God and the angels in an ancient script such as those used by the Hebrews, Greeks and Coptic Christians. It was believed that these scripts held great magical properties because of their antiquity.

In the 15th and 16th centuries, discovering ancient and exotic alphabets became popular intellectual pursuit among many European scholars, including Dr. John Dee, and a great undertaking took place as learned men sought to find the original language, alphabet and script used by the Hebrew patriarchs to record the tongue of Adam in the Garden of Eden before the Fall. They conceived that the original alphabet from which all others, ancient and modern have been derived are no more than three.

1. The Old Syrian, the first divine alphabet taught by God to Adam. This script is the calligraphic origin of the Ashuri script style or Assyrian Black Letter, the parent of most modern Middle Eastern scripts, also those magic scripts called Chaldean.
2. The Celestial, in which the books which Seth received from Heaven were written. Celestial script is cited as being the

main form of angelic communication with man and is often referred to as Angelic script.
3. The Alphabet of Enoch, brought down to Earth by the Archangel Gabriel, who also revealed it to Dee and Kelly who referred to it as Angelic or Adamic. It is called Enochian because he was supposedly the last man to use it.

Celestial / Angelic Scripts

It is perceived that angels prefer to communicate with mankind by writing and this has produced a sub-category of magical scripts referred to as Celestial and/or Angelic. In cabala, each Hebrew letter is a living angel that expresses God's voice in written form, and shapes the stars that form shapes that represent those letters. Celestial or Angelic writing was first revealed to mankind by angels, specifically the Watchers and mankind used these letters in the Garden of Eden.

Celestial and Angelic scripts were created and employed by various adepts to express their mystical knowledge, used as ciphers for Hebrew and Greek, to write the names of God and angels on seals, pentacles and talisman's. They were reproduced in a number of 15th–17th century grimoires and polygraphia's.

Bartolozzi's Biblioteca Magna Rabbinica lists 7 celestial scripts including the Celestial and Malachim, both published by Agrippa and both listed in the Key of Solomon. The invention of the 'Celestial' script is attributed to Agrippa. The similar looking 'Malachim' meaning 'angel', 'messenger' or 'regal', is the celestial script style used to write the Tables of Law given to Moses. As its name suggests, Malachim was believed to be used in angelic writings and all communication between heavenly beings and man. Its origins are considered a mystery.

In 1523, Abraham De Balmes published 'The Flock of Abraham' which contained an alphabet called Katav ever ha-nahar or Script beyond the River. Composed of Celestial charakteres, it was picked up by magic enthusiasts including Agrippa who republished it as 'Scriptura Transitus Fluvi' or 'Passing the River script'. It is also listed in the Table of Magic Alphabets in the Key of Solomon.

The name may refer to the passage of the Jewish people across the river Euphrates when they returned from Babylon to rebuild the temple at Jerusalem. Through the centuries it has been popular with secret societies and is still used by today's high-degree Freemasons, albeit in a limited way. It is commonly used in talismanic inscriptions.

The Writing of the Magi is a script said to have been invented by a 16th century alchemist called Theophrastus Baubastis von Hohenhiem, better known as Paracelsus. It was used by its inventor to engrave the names of angelic beings on talisman's for treating illness and protection.

The Theban alphabet is first mentioned by Johannes Trithemius in his 16th century Polygraphia and by Agrippa, a student of Trithemius. It has a one to one correspondence with the letters of the Latin alphabet, except for J and V. It is possible that it began life as a Latin cipher used by early 10th century alchemists to disguise the meaning of a text and to give it a mystical quality. The script is also called the 'Runes of Honorius' after its reputed inventor, Honorius of Thebes, and the 'witch's alphabet', after it was used in the Book of Shadows to write witches spells, inscriptions on knives and swords and other texts.

Enochian Script (Angelic, Adamic)

A number of scripts are called Angelic because they are often revealed to man, including Adam, by angelic beings. One such script is the 16th century Enochian alphabet of Dr. John Dee and Sir Edward Kelly, which they considered to be a true angelic language.

The Enochian alphabet was revealed to Dee and Kelly during 'scrying' sessions, when various texts and tables were revealed to them by angels. Scrying is a technique used to tell the future and involves gazing into a reflective surface to receive messages. It is documented that Dee and Kelly used certain objects such as a black obsidian mirror and a crystal ball to experience these visions.

When Kelly could not aptly imitate the character or letter as they were shown, they appeared on his paper in a light yellow colour which he drew in black and the yellow disappeared leaving the black letter. Dee's conversation with the angels says, "These letters represent the Creation of Man, and therefore must be in proportion. They represent the workmanship, wherewithal the soul of man was made like unto his Creator."

However, Dee never described the language used during the sessions as 'Enochian', preferring to call it 'Angelical' or 'Adamical', 'The Celestial Speech, the First Language of God-Christ' and particularly used by Adam in the Garden of Eden to name all of God's creatures.

The Enochian alphabet is used in the practice of Enochian magic. Its structure is based on an alphabetical cipher for an angelic language that is recorded using a unique script formed of 21 letters, neither capitals or lowercase, written from right to left as in Hebrew and may include accents.

There are three slightly different versions of the Enochian script. Dee's version was published first in the Five Books of the Mysteries. Kelly's version, the original and more acceptable was published in the Liber Loagaeth, Aleister Crowley produced a third.

The Enochian script style is a European hybrid, derived from the mixing of Assyrian Blackletter forms and those Uncial forms of the Egyptian and Ethiopian Coptic Church, a popular mystic fashion of the time, as typified by Dee's Enochian alphabet and the earlier 'Enochian' script of Pantheo's Voarchadmia. Alternatively, Enochian scripts can be a Torahanic calligraphic variant of the Hebrew alphabet.

Air
wind,
warmth,
Holy Spirit,
breath

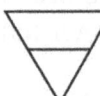
Earth
material,
movement,
physical sensations,
cool, dark

Water
female,
intuition,
moist, cold,
Baptisms

Fire
male, light
love, passion,
hate, anger,
moving energy to
reach the divine

Signs of the Elements

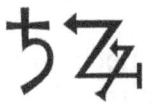
Saturn - Lead

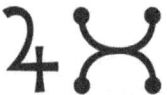
Jupiter - Tin

Mars - Iron

Sun - Gold

Venus - Copper

Mercury (Quicksilver)

Moon - Silver

Planetary Metals

Aries

Taurus

Gemini

Cancer

Leo

Virgo

Libra

Capricorn

Scorpio

Sagittarius

Aquarius

Pisces

Astrological Signs of the Zodiac

SYMBOLS AND SCRIPTS

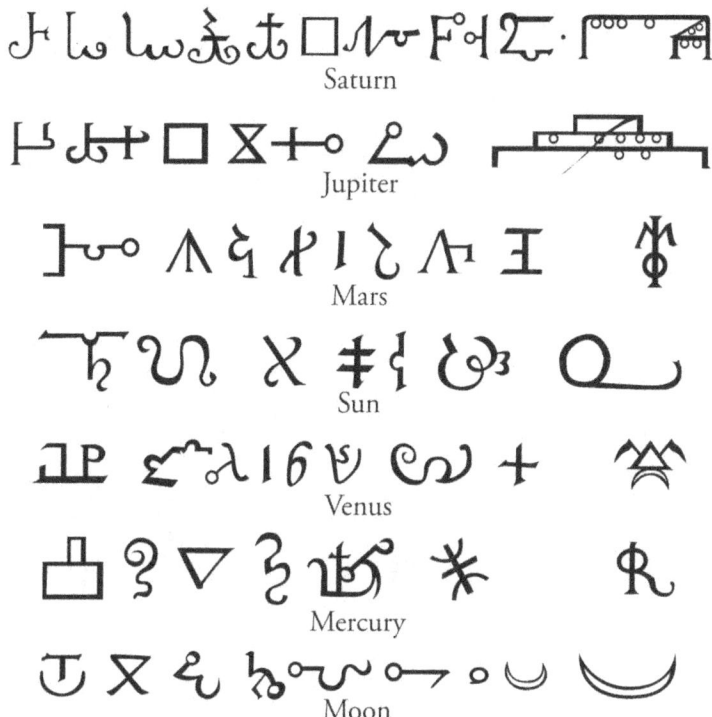

Planetary Characters - Lesser Key of Solomon / Ars Pauline

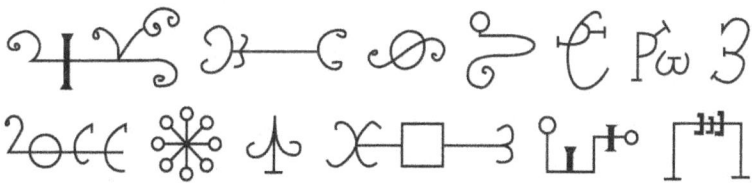

Magical characters marked in scarlet on a crown of virgin paper

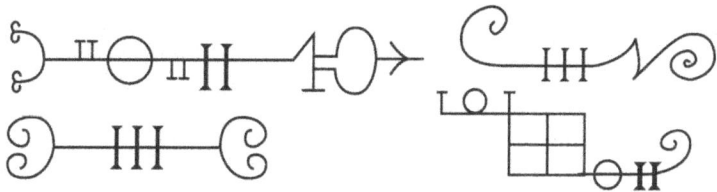

Characters to be embroided on the breast of a linen robe in red silk

Magical Characters - Lesser Key of Solomon / Ars Pauline

אבגדהוזחטיככלמם
M L   K I Th Ch Z V H D G B A

נןסעפףצץקרשת
T Sh R Q Tz P O S N

Classic Hebrew - Ktav Ashiri / Assyrian Black Letter

Α Β Γ Δ Ε Ζ Η Θ Ι Κ Λ Μ
α β γ δ ε ζ η θ ι κ λ μ
A B G D E Z E Th I K L M

Ν Ξ Ο Π Ρ Σ Τ Υ Φ Χ Ψ Ω
ν ξ ο π ρ σ τ υ φ χ ψ ω
N X O P R S T U Phi Ch Ps OO

Classic Greek Alphabet

Ⲁ Ⲃ Ⲅ Ⲇ Ⲉ Ⲋ Ⲍ Ⲏ Ⲡ Ⲣ Ⲥ Ⲧ
ⲁ ⲃ ⲅ ⲇ ⲉ ⲋ ⲍ ⲏ ⲡ ⲣ ⲥ ⲧ
A B,V G D E Ḝ Dz Ei P R S T

Ⲩ Ⲫ Ⲭ Ⲯ Ⲑ Ⲓ Ⲕ Ⲗ Ⲙ Ⲛ
ⲩ ⲫ ⲭ ⲯ ⲑ ⲓ ⲕ ⲗ ⲙ ⲛ
U Ph Kh PS Th I K L M N

Ⲝ Ⲟ Ⲱ Ϣ Ϥ Ϧ Ϩ Ϫ Ϭ Ϯ
ⲝ ⲟ ⲱ ϣ ϥ ϧ ϩ ϫ ϭ ϯ
Ks O U,O S F X H Dz Ts TI

(Egyptian) Coptic Uncial

Scripts with Magical Power from Antiquty

SYMBOLS AND SCRIPTS

יאע	IAO	IΔO	IΔO
Hebrew	Greek Capitals	Greek Uncial	Coptic Unci

IAO / JAO

יהוה	IHYH
Hebrew	Greek Capitals
IHYH	IϚⲰϚ
Greek Uncial	Coptic Uncial

IHVH - YaHWeH / Jahovah

סבבעאץ	ΣABBOAΘ
Hebrew	Greek Capitals
CΔBBOΔΘ	CΔBBOΔЄ
Greek Uncial	Coptic Uncial

SABBOATH

אדעני	AΔONAI
Hebrew	Greek Capitals
ΔΔONAI	ΔΔOHΔI
Greek Uncial	Coptic Uncial

ADONAI

Names of God - Greco-Egyptian Scripts

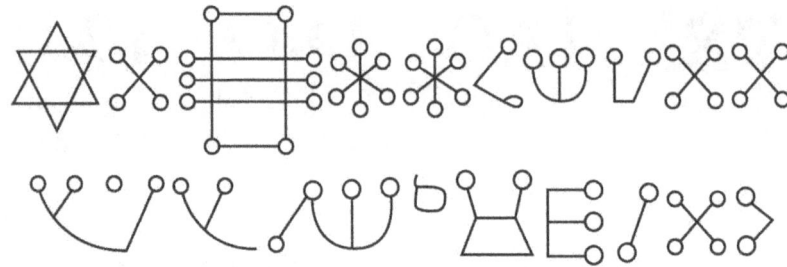

Charm written in Magical Charakteres for Grace and Favour

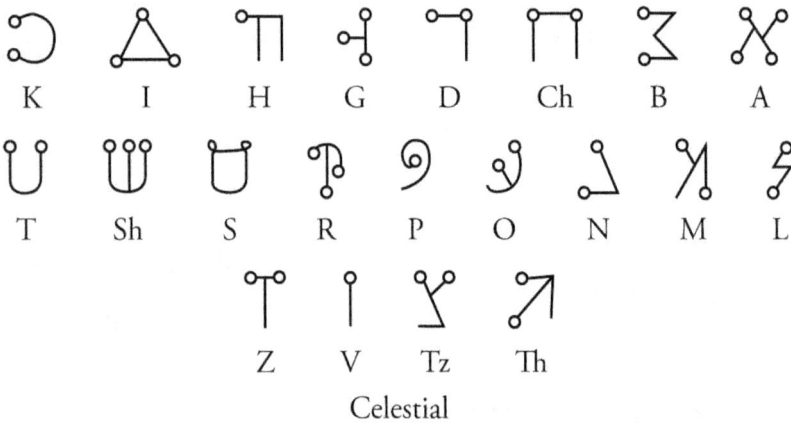

Celestial

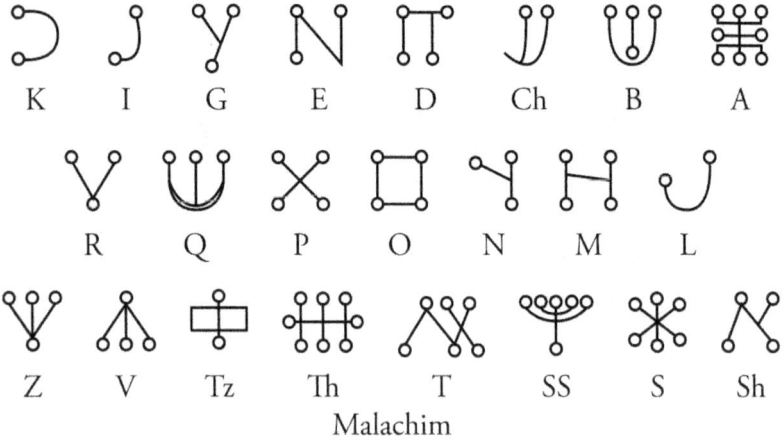

Malachim

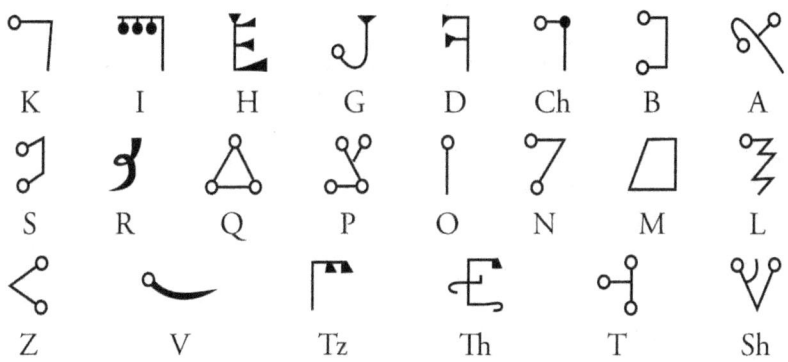

Scriptura Tranitus Fluvi / Passing the River Script

Celsestial / Angelic Hebrew Cipher Scripts - Agrippa

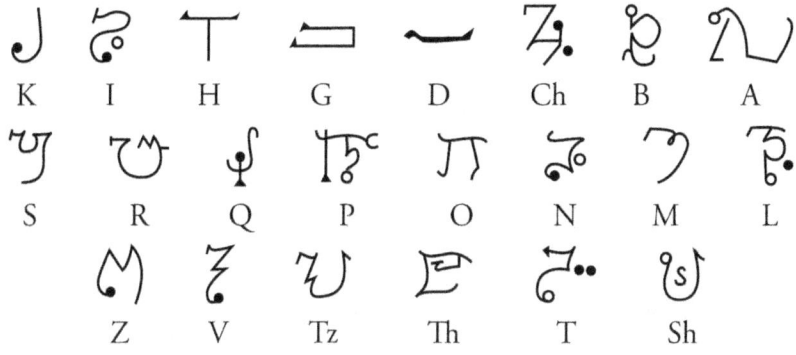

Writing of the Magi - for Hebrew names of Angels - Agrippa

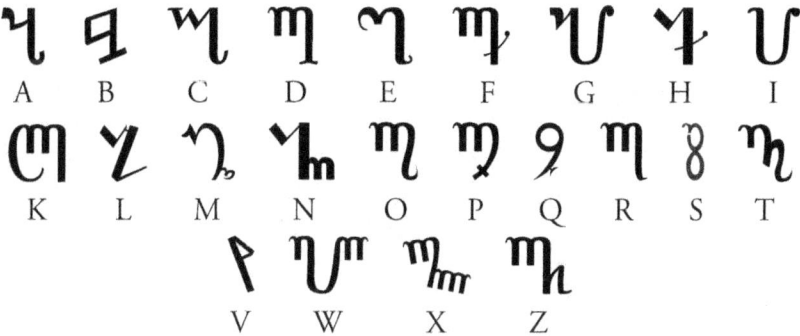

Theban / Runes of Honourius / Witches Alphabet - Agrippa

SIGILS, SEALS AND PENTACLES

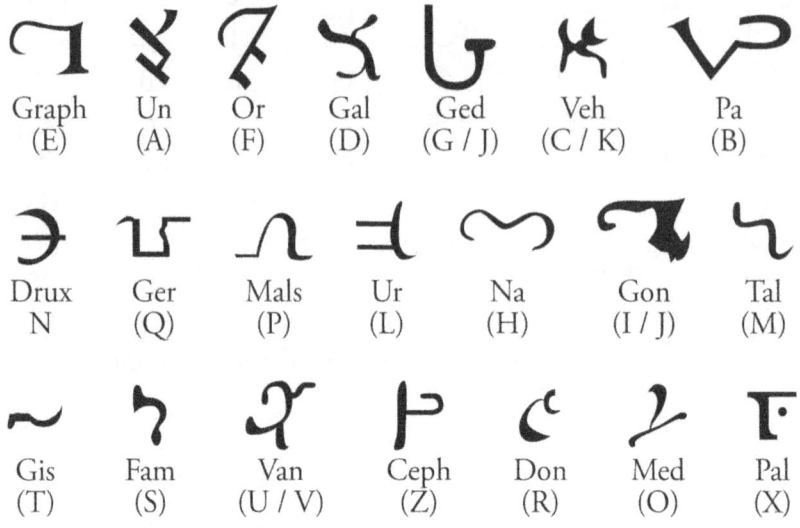

Dee's first version of the Angelic or Adamic Alphabet and Script

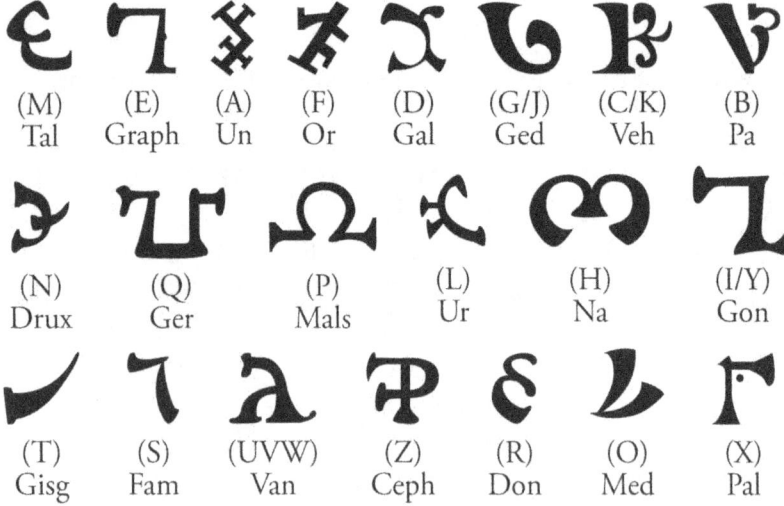

Edward Kelly's 'original' Enochian Alphabet (right to left)

SYMBOLS AND SCRIPTS

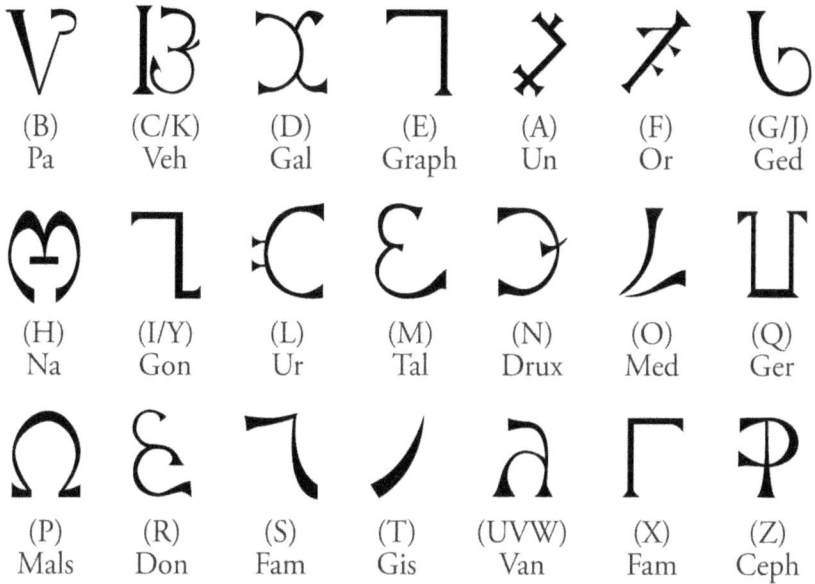

Aleister Crowely (left to right)

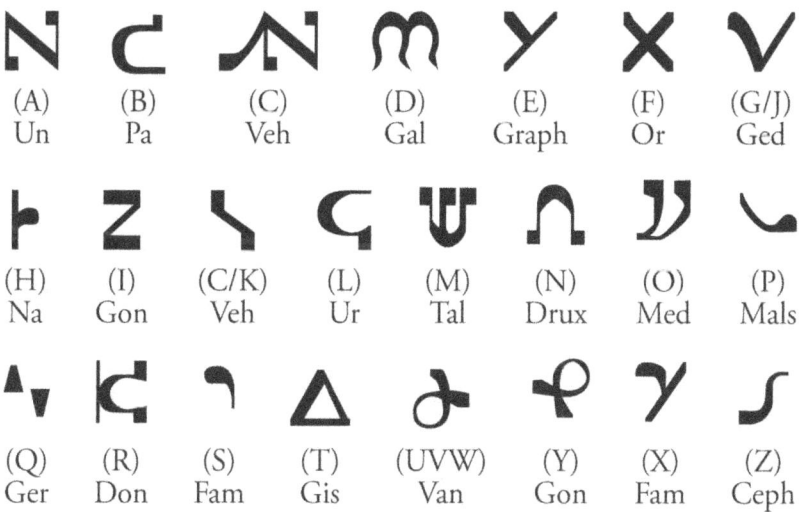

Voarchadumia - Pantheo (Encohian Style Script)

Angelic Spirits

Using symbols to control spirits is the primary reason sigils have existed for thousands of years. But the power of the sigil lies in the fact that an image can represent many different concepts or desires, this allows the conjurer to all upon different types of spirit. These entities can be classified into groups depending on their status and invoked for different reasons due to the nature of the spirit.

In the Medieval and Renaissance periods, the evocation of spirits was closely regulated by the Christian church. Occult scholars created lists of the names of angels and demons and their correspondences, giving them titles and ranks and only those from the Judeo-Christian tradition were cautiously allowed to be summoned, all other spirits were considered to be pagan.

In the Judeo-Christian tradition, celestial spirits are associated with the directions, elements, planets, archangels and those angels, spirits and intelligences thereof. Demonic spirits are associated with Satan, Lucifer, the Fallen Angels and the Infernal Hordes of Hell. Many of these entities names either begin or end in EL – ELohin, MichaEL, SamaEL – that denotes them as angelic entities, good or evil.

Cardinal Spirits
These are the spirits of the four directions and it is considered that these spirits are relatively easy to contact. They are often combined with the four elements which represent them. In the 'Simon' Necronomicon, there are the four cardinal spirits called the Spirits of the Spaces, in the north dwells Uster, a being of human form. In the east dwells Sed, a bull with a human face. In the south dwelleth Lamas who has a lion's body with a human head. In the west dwelleth Nattig who has a human body with the wings and head of an eagle.

Elementary Spirits

It is considered that these spirits are relatively easy to contact, if a magician has an understanding of the magical elements they represent. These intelligences are very specialized and unlike planetary spirits who often possesses many areas of knowledge, each element usually has only one area of expertise in which it is proficient.

Magicians work with elements to effect change in one's environment and circumstances. The four elements of Fire, Water, Air and Earth and their attributed qualities have been a fundamental part of western magic practice from the time of the ancient Greeks. In cabala, the spirits of the elemental spheres belong to the Archangel Sandalphon and the Sefira of Malkuth. The Enochian magic of the Golden Dawn evokes elemental spirits in the operations of the four Watchtowers.

Planetary Spirits

Planetary spirits are very powerful and can help the magician in a number of related tasks simultaneously. They are some of the easiest entities to work with and may be conjured using various sets of symbols. The most useful set of planetary symbols are those of the planetary kamea, as published by Agrippa.

Planetary kamea are magic squares used to draw in the influence of their corresponding planet. Each kamea represents a matrix of planetary energy. They are based on the original work done by ancient mathematicians in their description of numbers. Magic practitioners expanded on this to carry over correlations between a number and its corresponding planet, therefore representing planetary energy in a mathematical format.

A kamea is made up of three key numbers. The first is the planetary number. The second is the square of the planetary number, or the planetary number multiplied by itself. The third is the sum of the square or all the incremental numbers starting at one that it takes to fill the boxes in the square added together and divided by the planetary number.

Since there is only one possible square of three, the sigil of Saturn is made by connecting the numbers 1, 2, 3, 4, 5, 6; 7, 8, 9, with lines. For numbers larger than three, the rules of construction are divided into two groups, odd and even numbered squares. The even numbered squares are further subdivided into doubly-even squares, divisible by 4, and singly-even squares, divisible by two but not by 4. From on the process becomes even more complicated.

The Seven Wonders of the Ancient World are thought to be constructed from the geometry taken from the seven planetary kamea. The Colossus of Rhodes from the kamea of the Sun, the Temple of Diana at Ephesus from the Moon; the Great Pyramid from Mercury; the Tomb of Mausolas from Venus; the Hanging Gardens of Babylon from Mars; the Statue of Zeus from Jupiter; and the Lighthouse of Alexandria from Saturn.

Each individual planetary kamea contains a seal which is a geometric diagram designed so as to touch upon all the numbers of the square. Unfortunately, not all the seals follow the convention of overlapping every number in a kamea. Twelve numbers are missed in the seal of Venus, three are missed from Mars and some poor interpretations of the seal of the Moon don't include all the numbers.

The seal is the epitome or synthesis of the kamea and are used to block a planet's energy. By placing the seal of the planet over its kamea, it eliminates the retrograde or negative influences of the planet.

The planets seal was used for magical purposes only, especially in the preparations of amulets and talismans. In talismanic magic the seal is used to represent the entire pattern of the kamea and to act as a witness or governor for them.

Apart from the planetary seal there are two planetary sigils connected to each kamea. They are called the intelligence and the spirit which are derived from key numbers of the square using techniques of gematria. The intelligence of a planet is viewed as an evolutionary, guiding, inspiring or informing entity. The spirit is traditionally considered more of a blind or neutral force. Each intelligence and spirit has a sigil, which is considered an analogical glyph of the associated name, number, force, etc.

If the numerical equivalent of a letter does not exist on a given kamea, the number is reduced to the next lowest value in the same division of the Aiq Bkr cipher until it fits on to the kamea. The resulting numerical sequence is then traced on the appropriate kamea to produce the sigil of that name. Some traditional sigils do not follow the entire numerical sequence of each name. Some longer sigils seem to have been shortened or compressed for easier use.

Angels of the Hours of the Night and Day

When starting a magical operation, the magician must prepare all the requisite's, observing the days, hours and other effects of the constellations. It is desirable to know that the hours of the day and night number twenty-four and that each hour is governed by one of the seven planets in regular order – Saturn, Jupiter, Mars, Sun, Venus, Mercury, Moon. And the planets have dominion over the days of the week that it takes its name from – Saturday, Thursday, Tuesday, Sunday, Friday, Wednesday, Monday.

The rule of the planets over each hour begins from the dawn of the rising sun on the day which takes its name from such planet, and the planet that follows it in order succeeds to rule over the next hour. Note that each experiment should be performed under the planet and usually in the hour which refer to the same.

Angels of the Days of the Week

In the angel hierarchies of the Christian tradition there are three spheres of angels containing three orders or choirs of angels. Those closest to God appear in the first sphere in the order of Seraphim, Cherubim and Thrones. The second sphere contains Dominations, Virtues and Powers. The third sphere contains Principalities, Archangels and Angels. Archangels are the chief angels or first in rank and act as messengers or envoys.

The earliest reference to a system of seven archangels is in the Book of Enoch, their names being Gabriel, Michael, Raphael, Uriel, Raqael, Remiel and Saraqael. As well as their Hebrew names, there are also Christian and Islamic variants, leading to a divergence of correspondence among them.

Various occult systems associate numerological correspondences to each archangel. The system of seven archangels corresponds to the seven planets, seven days of the week, seven colours of the rainbow, seven notes on the musical scale, as well as having other properties. The system of twelve Archangels correspond to the astrological signs of the Zodiac. The Archangels are also linked to the Olympian and Black Venus spirits that are associated with the days of the week.

Olympian Spirits

Although no one is quite sure of their origin, Olympian sigils represent the names of seven, sometimes fourteen spirits. According to the 16th century magical ritual system known as Arabatel, the Olympian spirits are through whom God governs the world, from whence they get the name the Seven Stewards of the Heaven.

The Arbatel introduced these entities as the Olympian spirits, "which do inhabit the ferment, and in the stars of the ferment and the office of these spirits is to declare destinies, and to administer fatal charms, so for forth as God pleaseth to permit."

In this magic system, the universe is divided into 196 provinces with each of the seven Olympian spirits ruling a set number of provinces. The energies they rule correspond to the seven magical planets and therefore these beings are very similar to other planetary intelligences. Some differences between the two do exist, and in many ways the Olympian entities are more useful than most planetary ones. Each of the seven celestial spirits maybe invoked by the magician with the aid of ceremonies and preparations and are invoked in conjunction with the angels of the days of the week.

Black Venus Spirits

Another order of celestial spirits is found in the grimoire called the Black Venus by Dr. John Dee, who illustrates a set of sigils that correspond to the archangels ruling the planets, not the planetary gods themselves. These celestial spirits are not to be confused with the seven archangels. They are often invoked in conjunction with the archangels and magical seals often associated one of the spirits with one of the archangels.

The Black Venus sigils were collected by Dee on his travels through Europe. They are similar in construction to Olympian sigils and both are thought to be derived from the same archaic source, thought to date from before 3,000 BC, derived from central European Neolithic petrographs representing the planetary deities. It seems that their use was continued by Bronze age blacksmiths as alchemical symbols and thought to have become a part of the 'underground' Dark Goddess tradition of the Cathars and Rosicrucian's. The Black Venus manuscript fuses the high magic of the Renaissance with earlier practices of amalgamated Goddess traditions and the absorption of these traditions into mystical Christian and Jewish sects.

72 Angels of the Shamhamphorash

These Angels take their name from the cabalistic concept of Shemhamphorash or the 72-fold name of God, describing the hidden names of God. The 72 angels being the mystical name of God. Shem means Divine Name; the name is Tetragrammaton – YHWH, who is Supreme Lord of the 4 Elements or the Whole Universe.

Their names are divined from a special arrangement of 216 consecutive letters of the 3 verses numbered 19, 20 and 21, taken from Exodus, concerning a formula used by Moses to part the Red Sea. The formula is a key to the Sefer Raziel and a key component of the Lesser Keys of Solomon. It can also grant Holy men with the power to counteract demons.

The letters of the verses are written out to form triplets by taking the first letter of verse 19 – Vau, the last letter of verse 20 – Heh, and the first letter of the 21st verse – Vau, to make the first triplet – VHV. This is repeated to create the remaining names. The results provide the three consonants to form each of the 72 holy names. The three letter names of God become the names of angels by adding either IEL or IAH (Yah) to the end of each name.

The 72 angels primarily serve God and carry out missions from God to men, but many serve directly as Guardian Councilors, Guides, Judges, Interpreters, Cooks, Comforters, Matchmakers and Grave Diggers. Each angel has its own kamea on which its sigil and the sigils of their intelligences are found and its own set of magical characters.

In the ceremonial magic of King Solomon, the 72 angels protect the conjuror from the 72 goetic demons they are numerically paired with. Each angel controls and counters a specific demon, typically of the same number. There is a discrepancy in the demon's number system so it doesn't directly match up.

Sephirotic Angels

Sephirotic angels are forces that send information and sensation between mankind and the Tetragramaton or YHWH. Because of this, it is reasoned that they should not be worshipped, prayed to, nor invoked. When they appear, they are seen only from the viewpoint of the recipient, which will be anthropomorphic.

According to cabala as described by the Hermetic Order of the Golden Dawn, the Tree of Life illustrates how God the Creator expressed his creative energy throughout the Universe, through angels and on to human beings. Each of the tree's branches are called sephiroth, spheres that symbolize a particular type of creative force that a different archangel oversees. There are ten sephirotic archangels, each corresponding to one of the ten sephiroth.

Sephirotic angels are known for their work for justice and have no set or traditional sigil forms. The most important of the them is Metatron, the second most powerful being in the Universe after God himself. Sandalphon is considered the 'brother' of Metatron, he is the leader of the Ishism, those angels closest to humans.

The ten Archangels of the Holy Sephiroth are paired with 10 Unholy Sephira of the Qliphoth. Cabalistic demons are the incarnation of human vices, which derive from the Qliphoth, the representation of impure forces.

Enochian Spirits

Enochian is a unique form of Renaissance ceremonial magic allegedly transmitted by angels to Dr. John Dee, court astrologer to Queen Elizabeth 1, and clairvoyant Sir Edward Kelly, over a period of seven years beginning in 1581, using the technique of 'scrying' that involves the use of a reflective surface such as a crystal ball or black obsidian mirror to receive messages.

In 1584, Kelly scryed the names of the 91 Governors that make up the four quadrants that form the Great Table of Enochian magic. He was then given the names of the provinces of the world these Governors were supposed to control. They are supposed to influence particular parts of the world and their governments.

This Angelical system portrays the Universe in an image called the Great Table which is sited at the center of 30 concentric circles representing the 30 Aethyrs. The Great Table is a grid formed from a total of 675 lettered squares that was revealed to Kelly and Dee as four smaller tablets that form the four quadrants called Watchtowers. These four tablets are 12 x 13 lettered grids totaling 156 squares. Added together, they make 624 squares.

When the Watchtowers are properly aligned and bound by a tablet called the Black Cross of 51 lettered squares, they form the 675 lettered squared grid known as the Great Table. Once constructed, the Great Table is composed entirely of Enochian letters that reveal the names and the sigils of the 91 Governors that are ruled by the 30 spirits of the Aethyrs.

Each of the 30 Aethyrs is populated by 3 Governors except for one that has 4, totaling 91 Governers in all. Each Watchtower has 22 Governors, the same 91 Governors who define the Aethyrs also define Earth.

The names of the 91 Governors make up the letters of the four Watchtowers. They reveal the 91 palaces, regions of the astral realm connected to each of their earthly territories. The names of the 91 Governors are seven letters long and each of the 91 Governors names are formed by the letters their sigils connect on the Great Table, arranged like an interlocking puzzle piece, revealing the order of the world according to the ideal plan of God.

Because the Governors names were encoded, the angels made Dee and Kelly write the Tablets in English because the Enochian alphabet has neither capital or lowercase letters. Some letters are shown in capitals, some in lowercase and two of the letters per Watchtower are backwards. The Angels insisted that Dee should discover for himself how to use the cipher. After much effort, he realized that the capital letters represented the initial letter of the Governors names.

ANGELIC SPIRITS

The Great Table contains many spirit names encoded in and around the cross formations of the Watchtowers. Each grid is said to be occupied by a Great King, his Seniors and various angelic and demonic beings, who are invoked using Enochian Calls.

The Watchtowers are connected by a central 'Black Cross' of 51 lettered squares. This cross shaped table contains four names, but the left side and the bottom of the cross mirror the names. The Golden Dawn took the 51 squares of the Black Cross and reduced then to 20 squares to make the Table of Union that corresponds to the fifth element of spirit, ether or quintessence. The Table contains the highest name of spirit, EHNB, the purest spiritual force, representing the building of spirit or an actual glue between the elements.

Each Watchtower is sub divided into four quadrants by the Seniors Cross, formed by the 6th and 7th columns and the 7th row. The names of the Elemental Kings and the Seniors are found within it. Their names are found in a spiral wound around the the hub of the Seniors Cross on each quadrant. The names of six Seniors are found on the Seniors Cross of the four tablets, making 24 in all. They follow the Kings in the order of heirarchy, representing the planets. they are the equivalent of the 24 Elders who worship at the Throne of God.

Each Watchtower contains a second cross called the Calvary or Sephirotic Cross, formed by the 3rd column and 2nd row of each quadrant. It contains the names of two Angels, giving the names of eight angels per Watchtower making 32 Angels in all. The names of the Angels found on the Kerubic Square are formed from the the first letter in each square above the Calvary Cross and are permutated to provide 4 in total per quadrant, making sixteen in all.

There are 129 names of demons in the Great Table. The Archdemon KHORONZON dwells in the Great Outer Abyss, formed by seperating the Watchtowers from the Tablet of Union.

142 SIGILS, SEALS AND PENTACLES

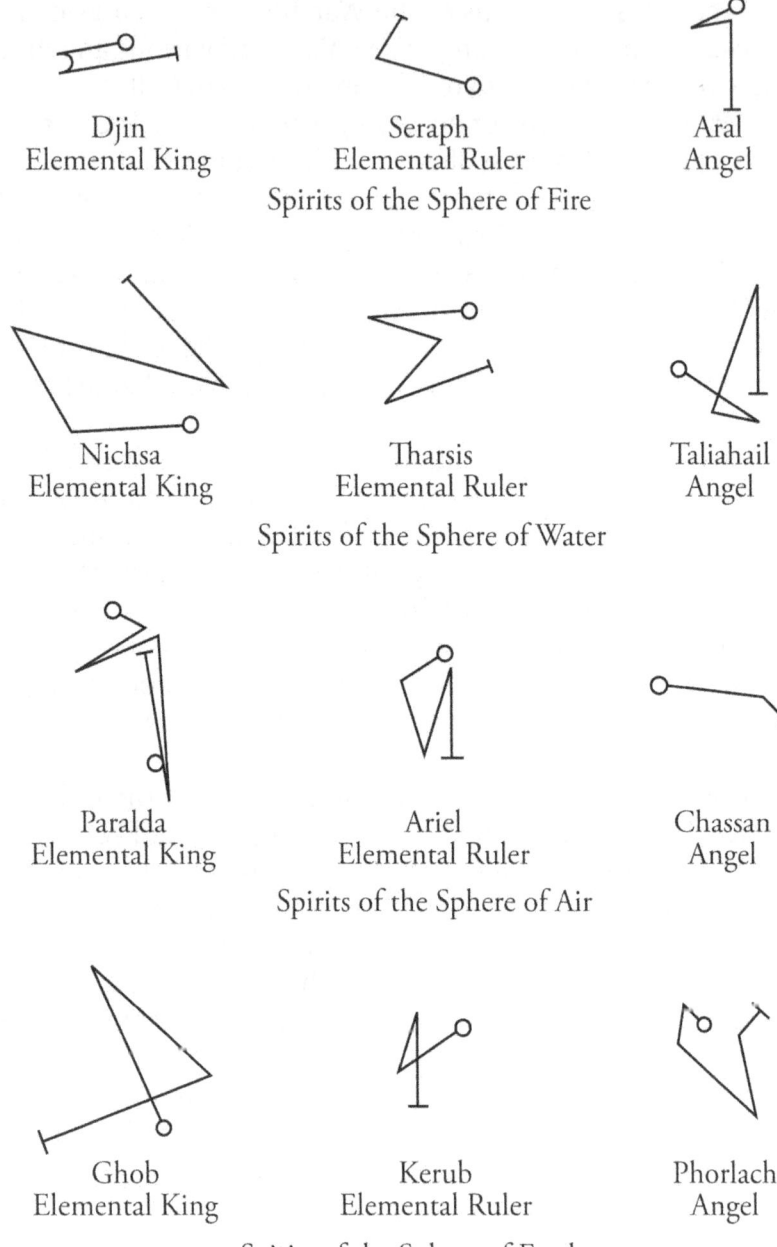

| Djin | Seraph | Aral |
| Elemental King | Elemental Ruler | Angel |

Spirits of the Sphere of Fire

| Nichsa | Tharsis | Taliahail |
| Elemental King | Elemental Ruler | Angel |

Spirits of the Sphere of Water

| Paralda | Ariel | Chassan |
| Elemental King | Elemental Ruler | Angel |

Spirits of the Sphere of Air

| Ghob | Kerub | Phorlach |
| Elemental King | Elemental Ruler | Angel |

Spirits of the Sphere of Earth

Spirits of the Elementsl Spheres

ANGELIC SPIRITS

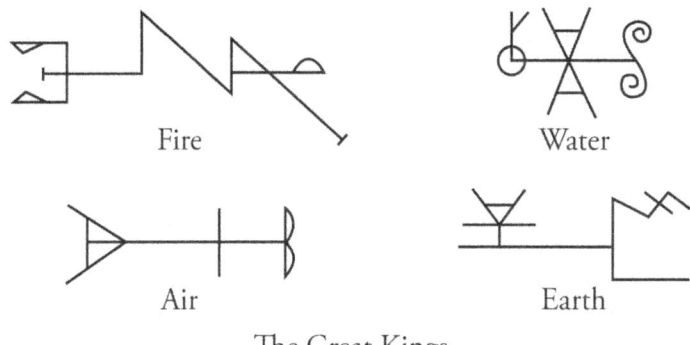

Fire

Water

Air

Earth

The Great Kings

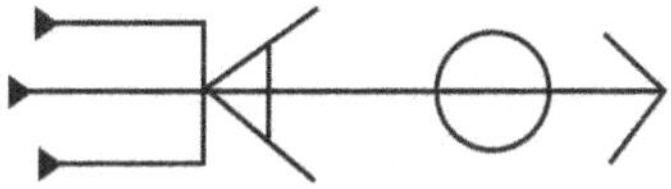

Fire

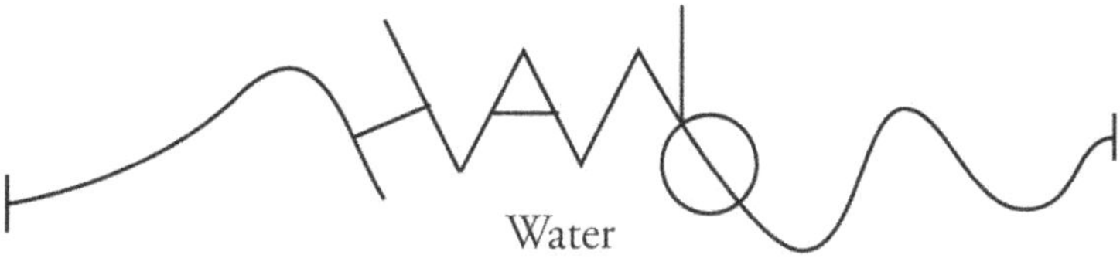

Water

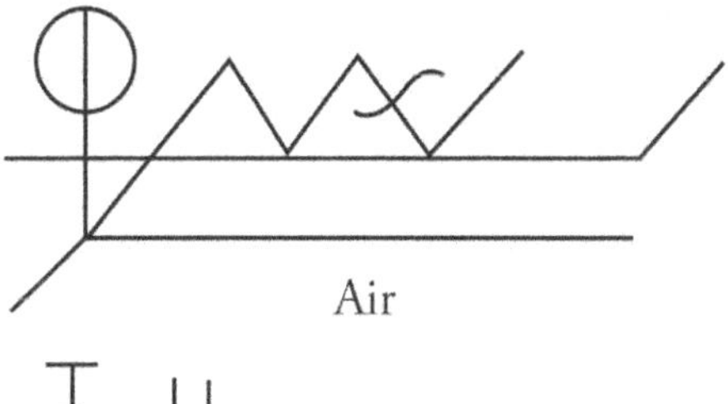

Air

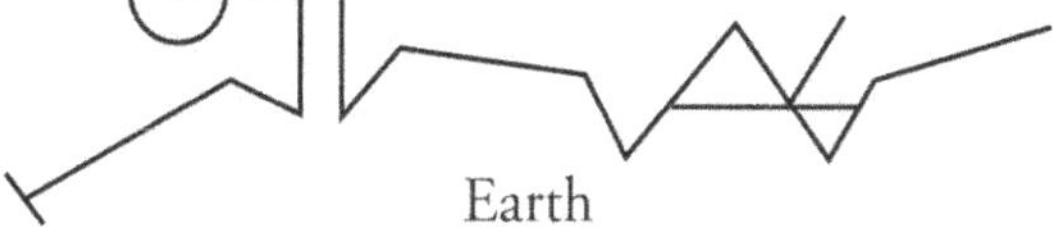

Earth

The Secret Holy Names

Enochian Elementsl Sigils - Golden Dawn

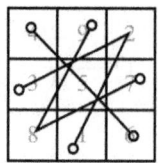

spirit
ZAZEL

inteligence
AGIEL

Seal of Saturn
3x3 magic constant 15 (3x15) 45

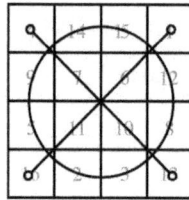

spirit
HISMAEL

inteligence
YOPHIEL

Seal of Jupiter
4x4 magic constant 34 (4x34) 136

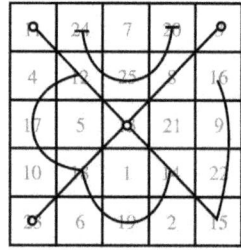
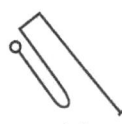

spirit
GRAPHIEL

inteligence
BARTZABEL

Seal of Mars
5x5 magic constant 65 (5x65) 325

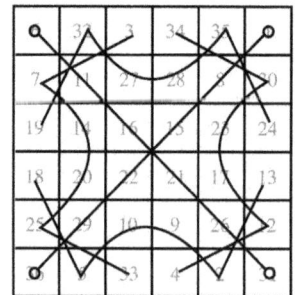

inteligence
NAKIEL

spirit
SORATH

Seal of the Sun
6x6 magic constant 111(6x111) 666

ANGELIC SPIRITS

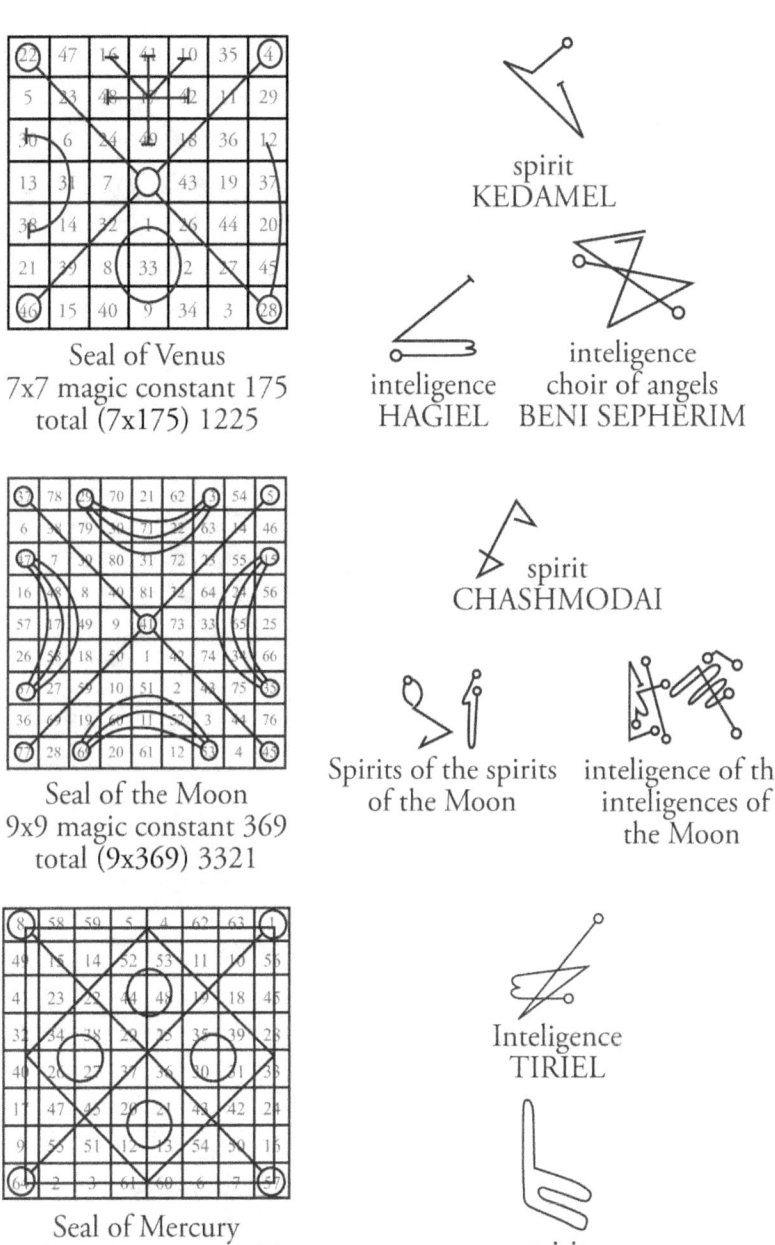

Seal of Venus
7x7 magic constant 175
total (7x175) 1225

spirit
KEDAMEL

inteligence
HAGIEL

inteligence
choir of angels
BENI SEPHERIM

Seal of the Moon
9x9 magic constant 369
total (9x369) 3321

spirit
CHASHMODAI

Spirits of the spirits
of the Moon

inteligence of the
inteligences of
the Moon

Seal of Mercury
8x8 magic constant 64
total (8x64) 2080

Inteligence
TIRIEL

spirit
TAPHARTHARATH

Planetary Kamea, Seals and Sigils - Agrippa

SIGILS, SEALS AND PENTACLES

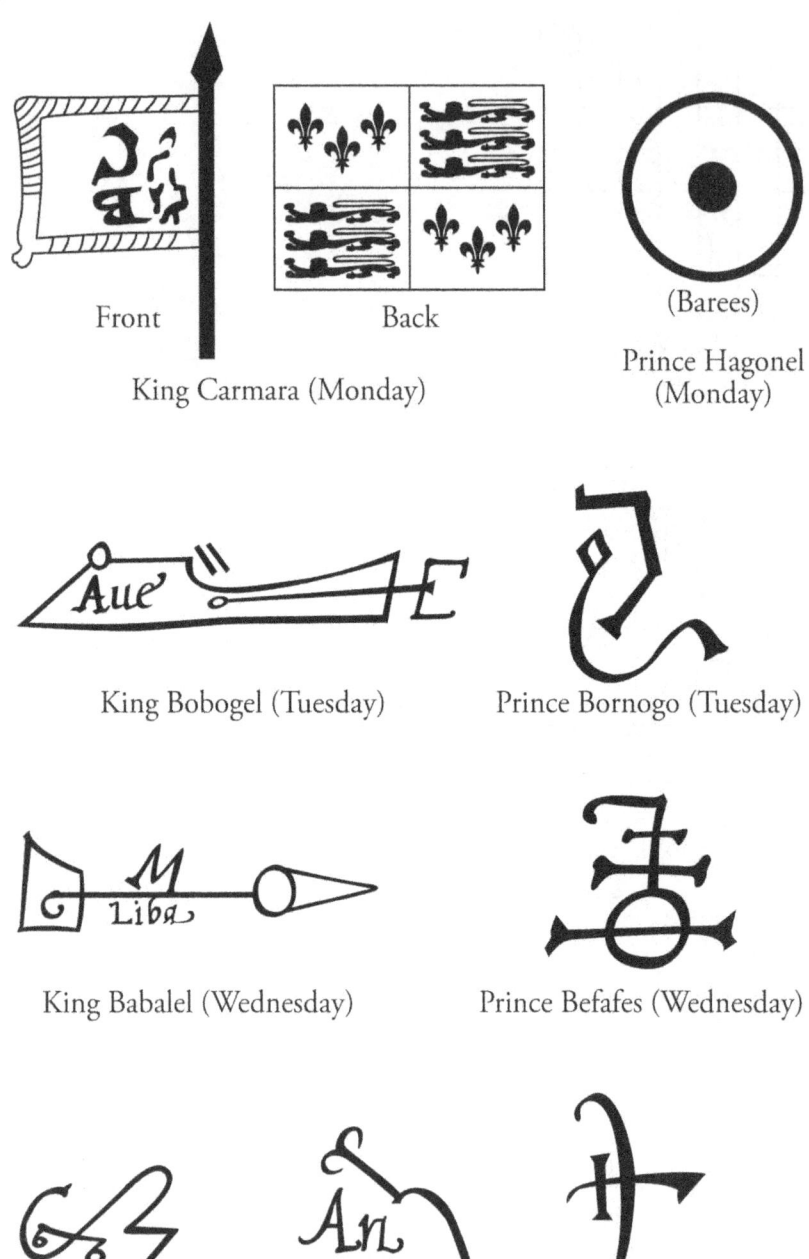

ANGELIC SPIRITS

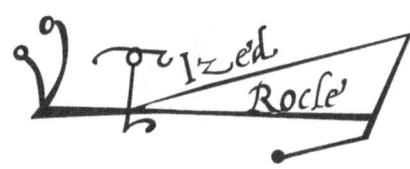 

King Bynepor (Thursday)   Prince Butmono (Thursday)

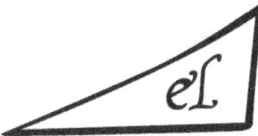

King Baligon (Friday)

Prince Bagend (Friday)
"no sigiil avaiable"

King Blavmaza (Saturday)   Prince Bralges (Saturday)

King Hagonel (Sunday)   Prince Brorges (Sunday)

Kings and Princes of the Days of the Week - Heptarchia

14 Dukes of the Day

ANGELIC SPIRITS

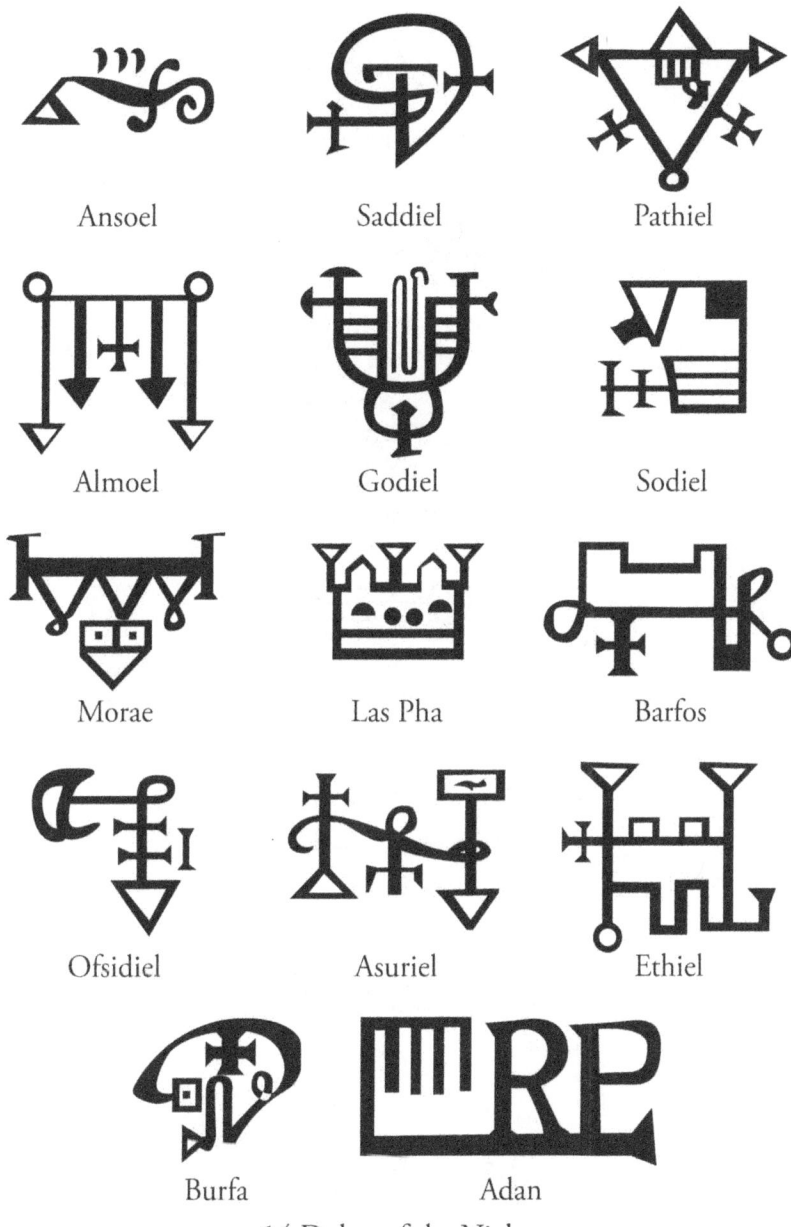

14 Dukes of the Night

Chief Spirit Usiel with his Ministry of Spirits of the Day and Night
Lesser Key of Solomon - Ars Theurgia Goetia

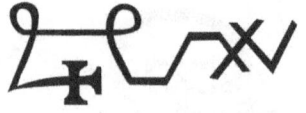
Michael - Sunday

Gabriel - Monday

Samuel - Tuesday

Raphiel - Wednesday

Sachiel - Thursday

Anniel - Friday

Cathiel - Saturday

'Luminary' Sigils of the Angels of the Days of the Week

ANGELIC SPIRITS

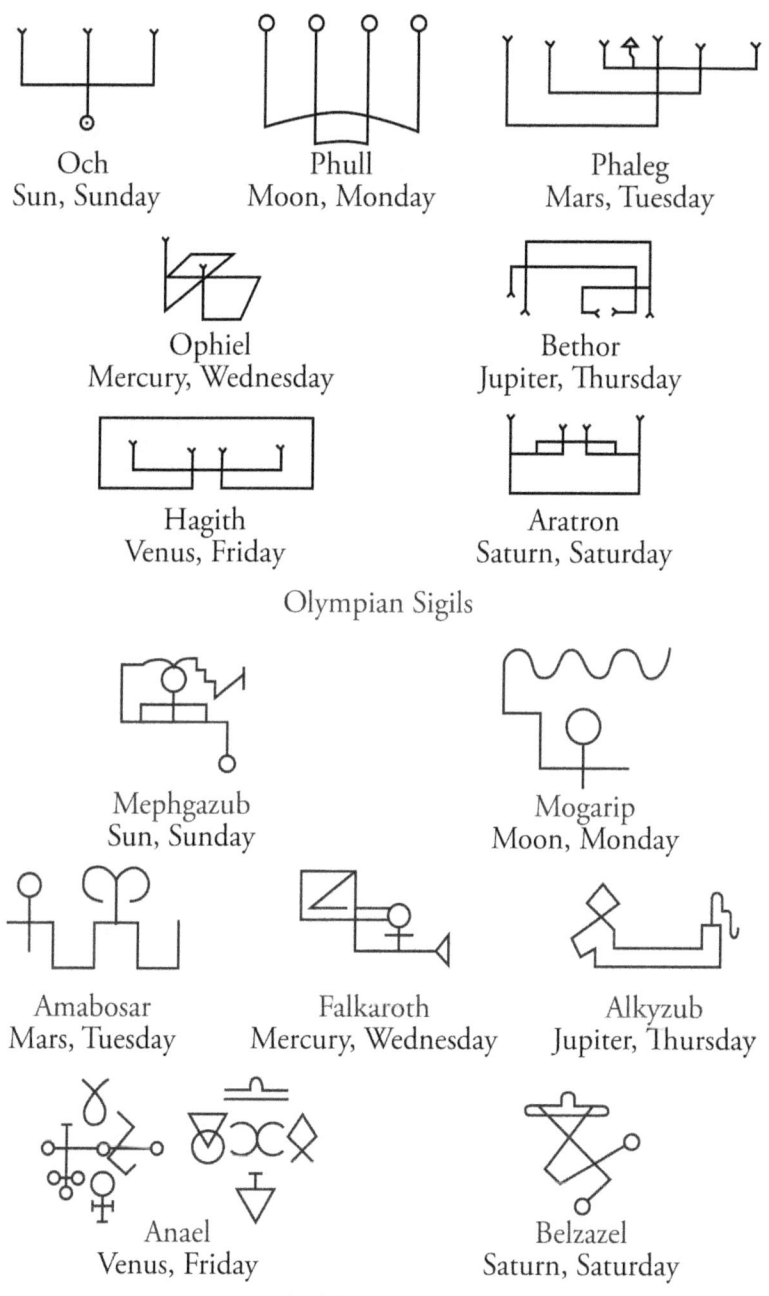

Och
Sun, Sunday

Phull
Moon, Monday

Phaleg
Mars, Tuesday

Ophiel
Mercury, Wednesday

Bethor
Jupiter, Thursday

Hagith
Venus, Friday

Aratron
Saturn, Saturday

Olympian Sigils

Mephgazub
Sun, Sunday

Mogarip
Moon, Monday

Amabosar
Mars, Tuesday

Falkaroth
Mercury, Wednesday

Alkyzub
Jupiter, Thursday

Anael
Venus, Friday

Belzazel
Saturn, Saturday

Black Venus Sigils

SIGILS, SEALS AND PENTACLES

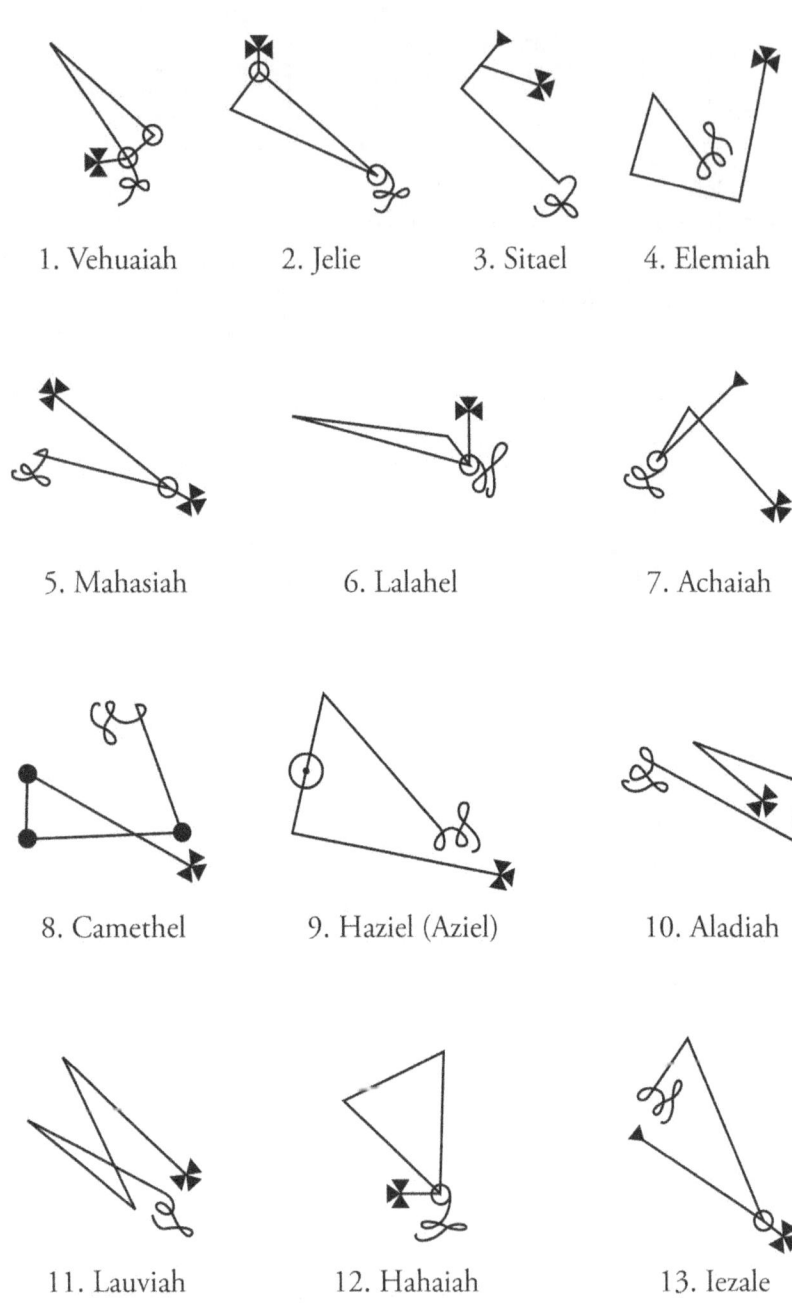

1. Vehuaiah   2. Jelie   3. Sitael   4. Elemiah

5. Mahasiah   6. Lalahel   7. Achaiah

8. Camethel   9. Haziel (Aziel)   10. Aladiah

11. Lauviah   12. Hahaiah   13. Iezale

Angels of the Shemhamphorash

ANGELIC SPIRITS

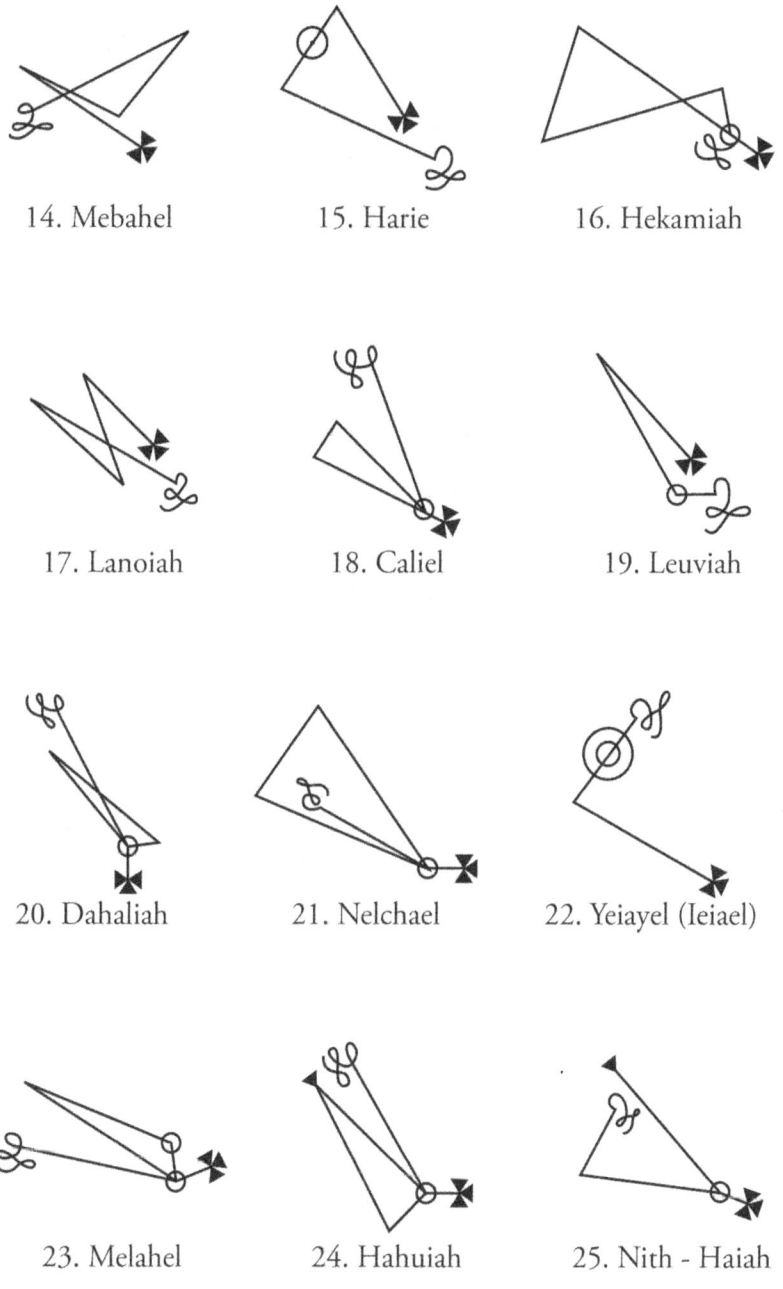

14. Mebahel 15. Harie 16. Hekamiah

17. Lanoiah 18. Caliel 19. Leuviah

20. Dahaliah 21. Nelchael 22. Yeiayel (Ieiael)

23. Melahel 24. Hahuiah 25. Nith - Haiah

Angels of the Shemhamphorash

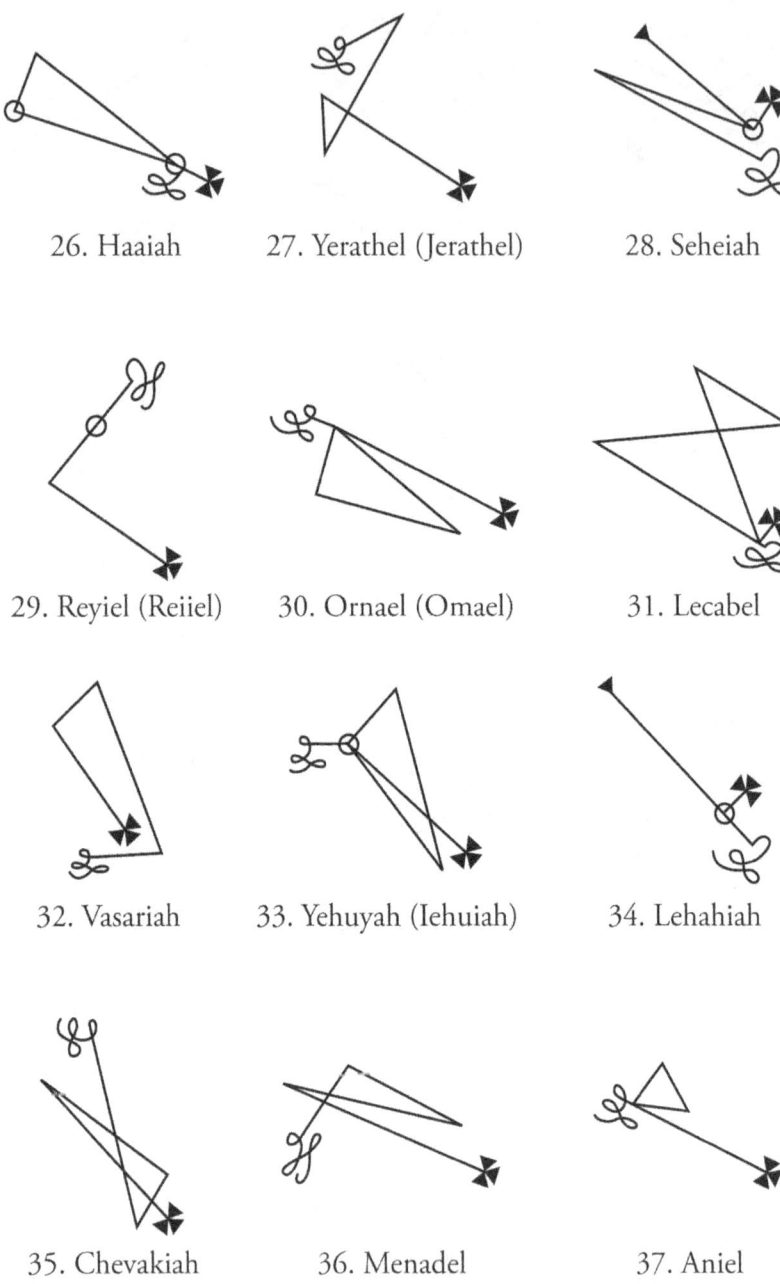

Angels of the Shemhamphorash

ANGELIC SPIRITS

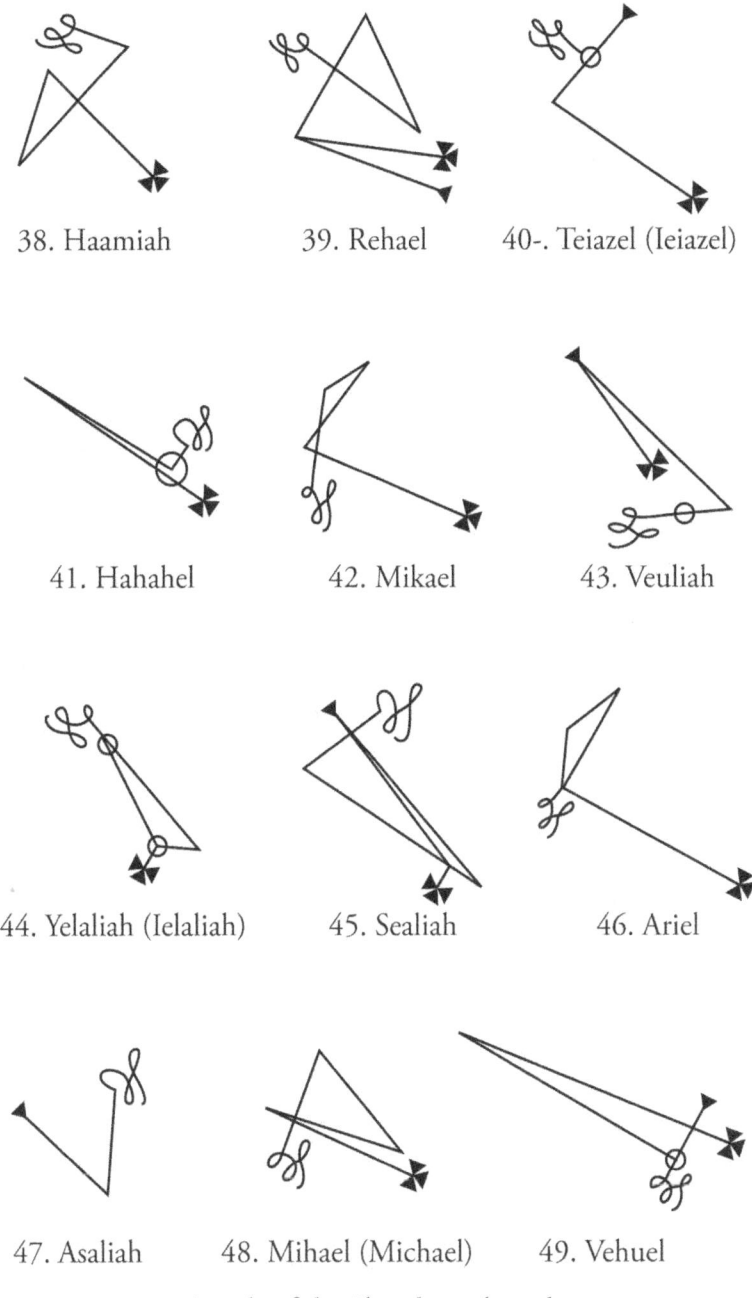

38. Haamiah   39. Rehael   40-. Teiazel (Ieiazel)

41. Hahahel   42. Mikael   43. Veuliah

44. Yelaliah (Ielaliah)   45. Sealiah   46. Ariel

47. Asaliah   48. Mihael (Michael)   49. Vehuel

Angels of the Shemhamphorash

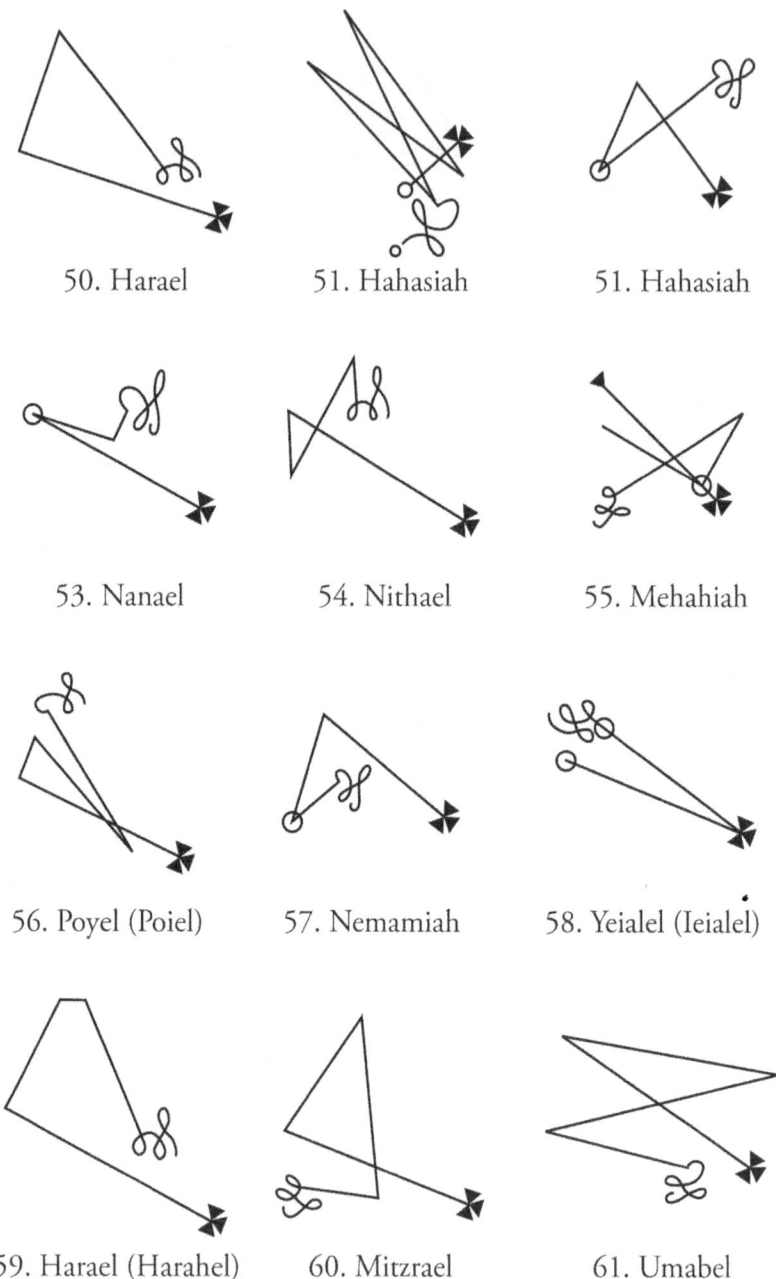

50. Harael 51. Hahasiah 51. Hahasiah

53. Nanael 54. Nithael 55. Mehahiah

56. Poyel (Poiel) 57. Nemamiah 58. Yeialel (Ieialel)

59. Harael (Harahel) 60. Mitzrael 61. Umabel

Angels of the Shemhamphorash

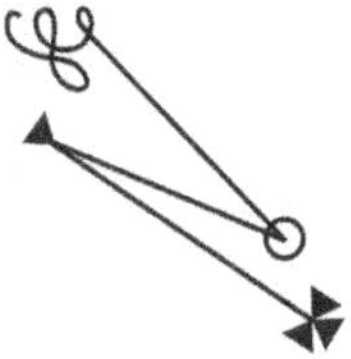

ANGELIC SPIRITS

62. Iah-El (Iah-Hel)  63. Ananel (Anianuel) 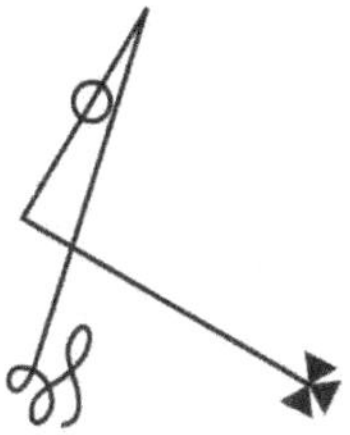 64. Mehiel

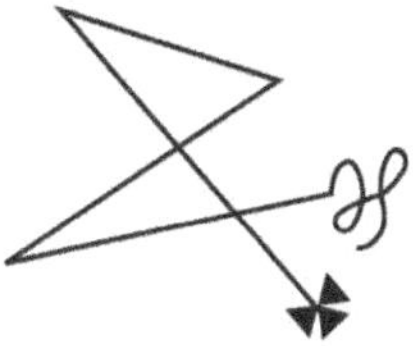

65. Damabiah 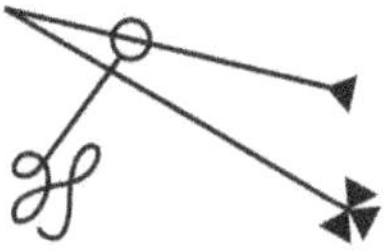 66. Manakel 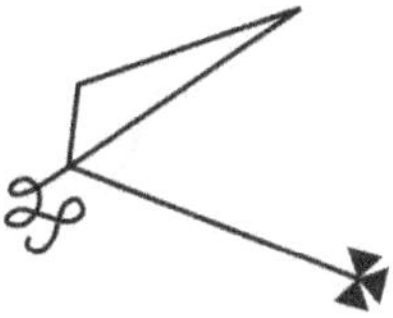 67. Eyael (Itaiel)

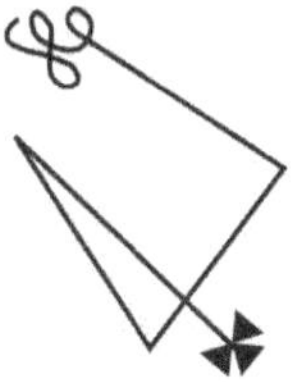

68. Mabuhiah / Chabuhiah 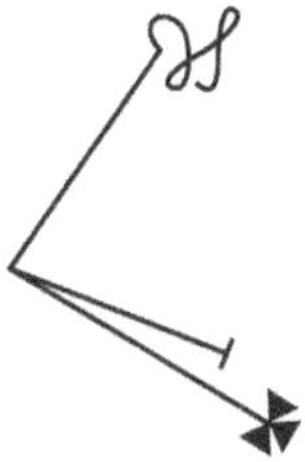 69. Rochel 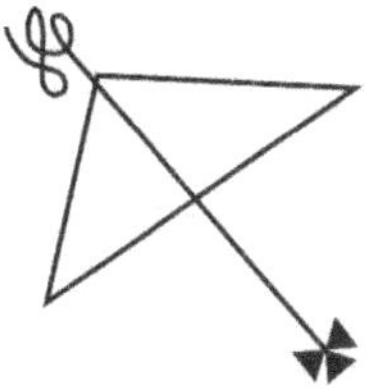 80. Jabamiah (Iabamiah)

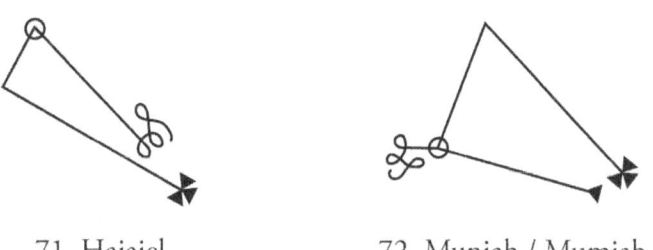

71. Haiaiel 72. Muniah / Mumiah

Angels of the Shemhamphorash

SIGILS, SEALS AND PENTACLES

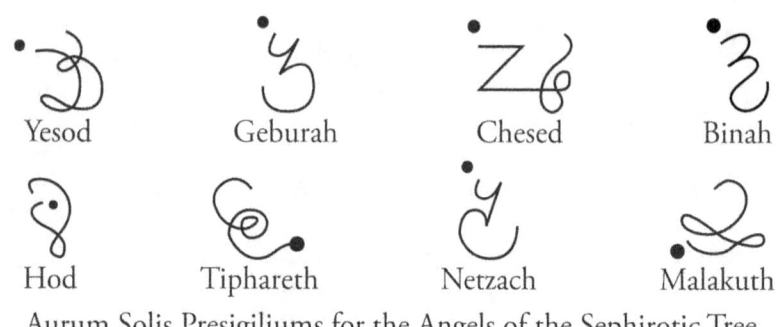

| Yesod | Geburah | Chesed | Binah |
| Hod | Tiphareth | Netzach | Malakuth |

Aurum Solis Presigiliums for the Angels of the Sephirotic Tree

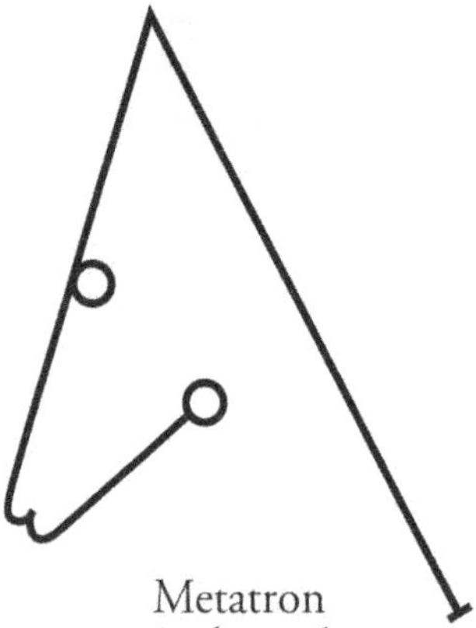

Metatron
Archangel
Kethor
Uranus

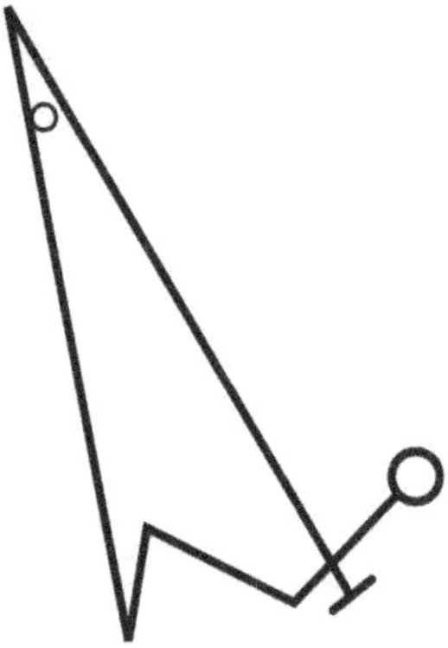

Sanfalphom
Archangel
Malkuth

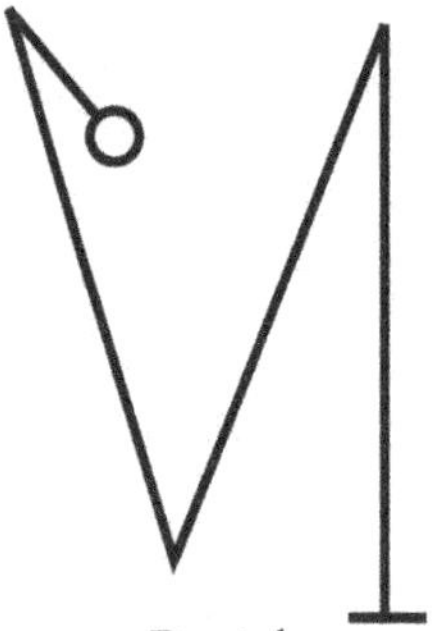

Raziel
Archangel
Chokmah
Neptune

Tzaphqiel
Archangel
Binah
Saturn

Tradqiel
Archangel
Chesed
Jupiter

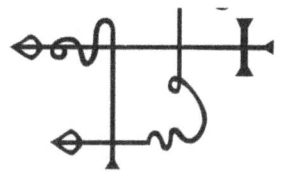

Kamael
Archangel
Geburah
Mars

Raphael
Archangel
Tipharech
Sun

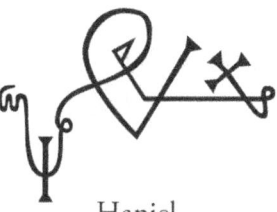

Haniel
Archangel
Netzach
Venus

Michael
Archangel
Hod
Mercury

Gabriel
Archangel
Yesod
Moon

Sigils of the Sephirotic Angels - Golden Dawn

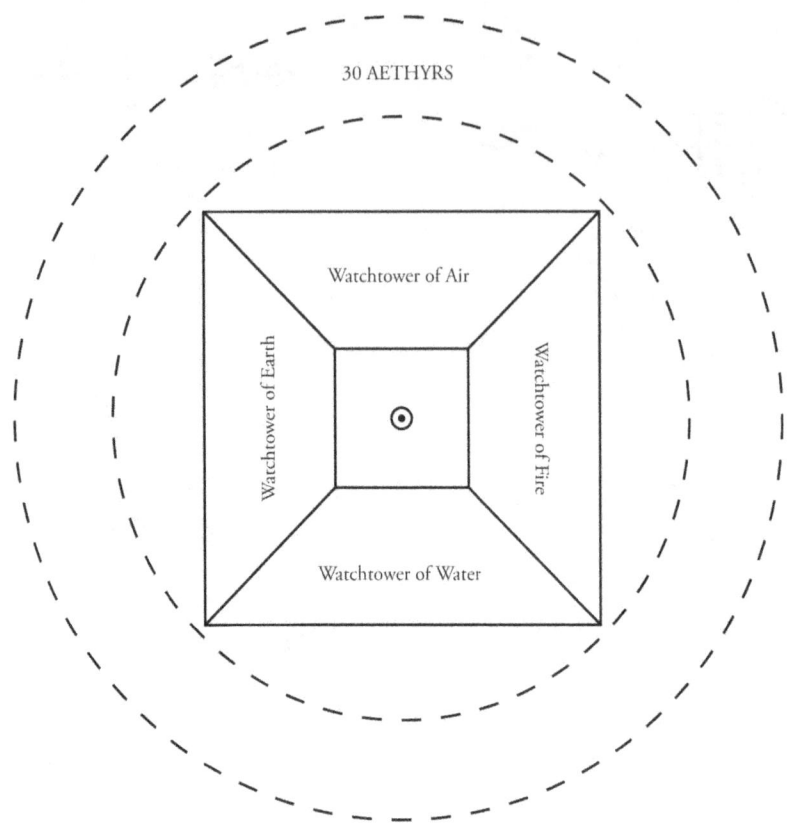

Elemental Watchtowers of the Great Table and the 30 Aethyrs

ANGELIC SPIRITS

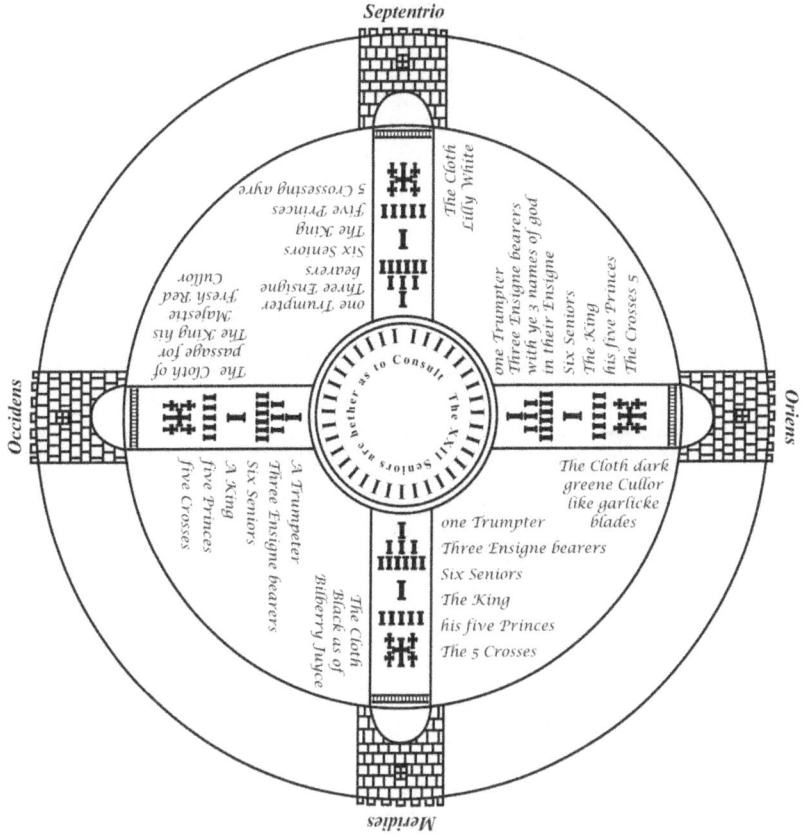

Dr John Dee's vision of the Watchtowers

Enochian Alphabet and the Great Table of Raphael

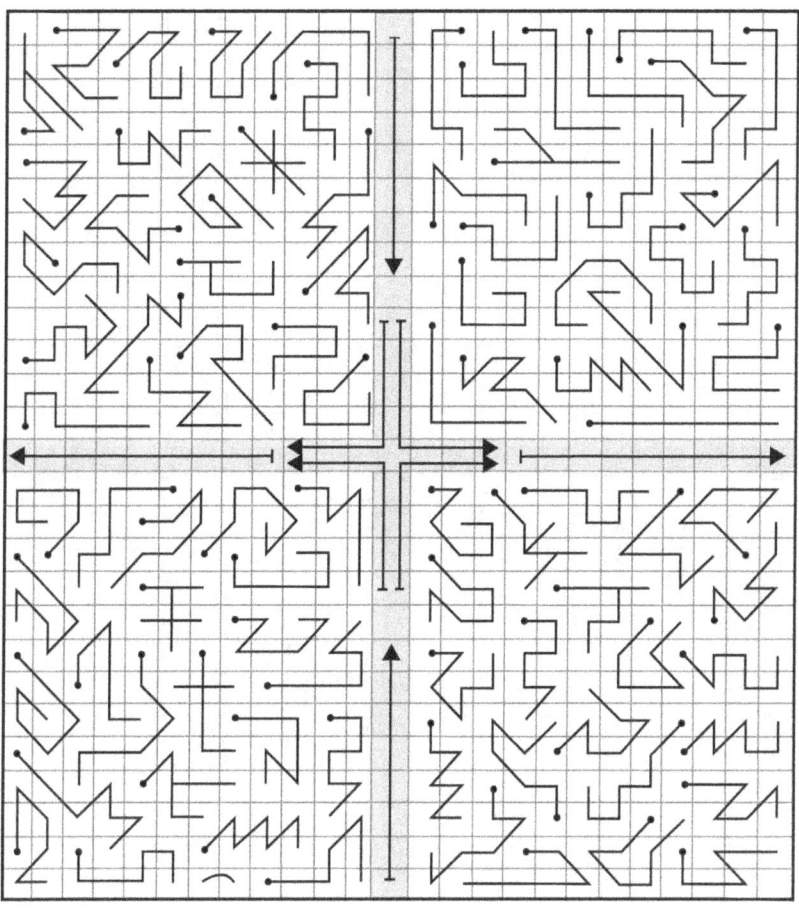

Sigils of the 91 Govenors on the Enochian Great Table

r	Z	l	l	a	f	A	y	t	l	p	a	o	b	O	a	Z	a	R	o	o	h	a	R	a
a	r	d	Z	a	l	d	P	a	L	a	m		u	N	n	a	z	o	P	S	o	n	d	n
o	z	o	n	z	a	r	o	Y	a	u	b	x	a	i	g	r	a	n	o	v	m	g	g	g
T	o	l	t	l	z	o	P	a	o	o	C	s	o	r	p	m	n	i	n	g	b	e	a	l
S	l	g	a	a	o	m	r	b	z	n	h	r	f	s	O	n	i	Z	i	r	l	e	m	u
l	m	o	n	d	o	T	d	i	a	r	l	p	l	z	l	n	r	C	z	i	i	M	h	l
o	r	o	l	o	A	h	a	o	z	p	i		M	O	r	d	i	a	l	h	C	r	G	a
i	N	a	o	r	V	i	x	o	a	s	d	h	O	C	a	n	c	h	l	e	z	o	m	l
O	i	l	i	i	T	p	a	l	O	n	i		A	r	b	i	z	m	i	i	f	p	i	z
A	b	u	m	o	o	o	a	o	u	c	a	C	O	P	a	n	n	L	a	m	S	m	a	P
N	a	o	c	O	T	t	n	p	p	n	T	o	d	O	l	o	p	i	n	i	a	h	b	a
o	c	a	n	m	a	g	o	t	t	o	l	m	r	x	p	a	o	e	s	l	z	i	x	p
S	h	i	a	l	r	a	p	m	m	o	x	e	z	y	f	i	r	V	g	e	t	r	i	m
m	o	t	i	b			o	t	n	a	n		n	a	n	T	n			b	l	t	o	m
T	a	O	A	d	u	p	t	O	n	n	m	a	d	o	o	p	a	T	d	a	n	V	a	a
a	a	b	c	o	o	r	o	m	o	b	b		o	l	o	n	G	o	o	o	b	a	u	a
T	a	g	c	o	n	x	m	a	l	G	m	m	O	P	a	m	n	o	V	O	m	d	n	m
n	h	o	d	D	l	a	l	e	a	o	n	o	a	p	l	o	T	e	d	e	e	a	o	p
P	a	t	a	x	i	o	V	s	p	i	N	O	s	c	m	i	c	o	n	A	m	l	o	X
S	a	a	l	x	a	a	r	y	r	o	l	h	V	s	r	s	G	d	L	b	r	i	a	p
m	p	h	a	f	g	l	g	a	i	o	l		o	o	P	t	e	a	g	p	D	c	c	e
M	a	m	g	l	o	i	n	L	l	i	X	o	p	a	u	s	c	n	r	Z	I	r	Z	a
c	i	a	a	Q	n	g\	a	t	a	p	a		S	l	o	d	a	o	i	n	r	z	f	m
p	a	l	c	o	i	d	x	P	a	c	n	r	d	a	l	f	T	d	n	a	d	l	f	o
n	d	e	z	N	z	i	V	a	o	e	a	a	d	i	x	o	m	u	n	g	i	o	s	p
l	d	d	P	o	h	o	d	A	s	P	i	x	O	o	D	p	z	l	A	P	a	n	l	l
a	i	i	n	h	t	a	s	P	d	i	L	o	r	g	o	a	n	n	P	A	C	r	a	r

English Translation of the Enochian Great Table

ANGELIC SPIRITS

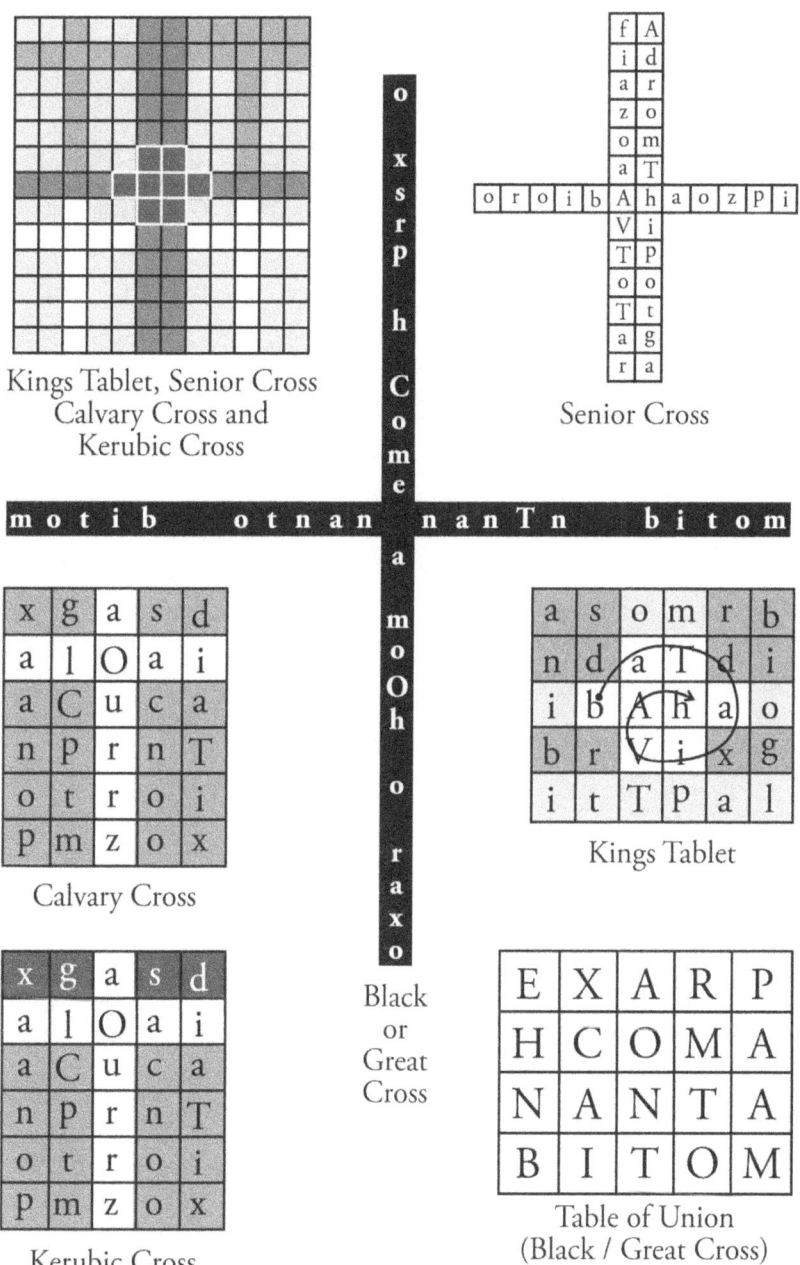

Crosses and Tablets found in the Watchtowers and Great Table

Demonic Spirits

Belief in demons goes back many millennia, Zoroastrianism teaches that there are 3,333 demons, some with specific dark responsibilities such as war, starvation, sickness, etc. Some believe these concepts are received as part of the cabalistic tradition. Others perceive demons were part of healing magic used to describe medical conditions such as epilepsy and mental illnesses.

Some scholars suggest the origin of early demonology can be traced to two distinct mythologies of evil – Adamic and Enochic. The Adamic story traces the source of evil to Satan's transgression and the fall of man. The Enochic tradition bases its demons on the story of the Fallen Angels led by Azazel. Enochic demons are derived from the names of the Fallen Angels listed against their transgressions written in the Book of Enoch.

The Fallen Angels come from all the orders of angels. They first disobeyed God when 200 of them gathered on a mountain top and married the daughters of Adam. They taught the sons of Adam all forms of forbidden knowledge from herbal medicine to metallurgy, warfare, reading, writing, astrology and divination. They were thrown out of Heaven when their leader 'Satan' tried to become equal in rank with God's power.

In the Sefer Zohar, God puts the Fallen Angels in chains, but they still copulate with the demoness Naamah, who gives birth to demons, evil spirits and witches. Besides tempting humans to sin, the Fallen Angels or devils were viewed as agents of famine, disease, war, earthquakes, accidental deaths, and various mental and various health disorders. Those suffering from mental illness were considered to be 'possessed by demons'.

The Christian church held that the world was pervaded with spirits and advanced the belief that demons received worship directed at pagan gods. A number of authors throughout Christian history have written about demons. Some Medieval scholars of demonology ascribed to a hierarchy of seven arch demons of the seven deadly sins, Lucifer – Pride, Mammon – Avarice, Asmodeus – Lechery, Satan – Anger, Beelzebub – Gluttony, Leviathan – Envy, Belphegor – Sloth.

Things that make a being into a demon are the mention of said being in the Bible, as in competition with God for worshippers. A connection with fertility, sexuality and sensuality, which the Christian church was particularly wary of. A connection with death and the underworld or a connection with the end of the world and ultimate destruction. By the Renaissance demons had become a mixture of Greek, Jewish, Christian, Arabic and other traditions which is why their names vary according to each grimoire.

Texts like the Pseudomonarchia Daemonum and the Lesser Keys of Solomon were written with instructions on how to summon demons in the name of God. These texts were usually more detailed, giving names, ranks and descriptions of demons. The ranks given to the spirits, Emperor, King, Prince, Duke, Marquis, Count, Knight, are European in origin and were in command of minor demons known as infernal hordes or servitors, to do their masters bidding.

The goetic demons of the Renaissance have a history beginning with a French grimoire of the 15th century titled Livre Des Esperitz or the Book of Spirits that feature 47 demons, 30 of which are reproduced in Johannes Wayer's Pseudomonarchia Deamonum, that features 60 of the 72 demons of the Ars Goetia found in the Lesser Keys of Solomon. Some of the number, names and sigils of demons featured by Agrippa and Kircher differ to those of the Lesser Keys of Solomon, although they are in essence the same Enochic spirits.

The 16th century text book titled Grimorium Verum or the Grimoire of Truth, first documented three Great Dukes of Hell, Emperor Lucifer, Prince Beelzebub and Grand Duke Astaroth as the evil three, the Chief Demons of Hell. They had six subordinate spirits, each with 17 corresponding subordinate spirits.

In 1969, Anton LeVey founder of the Church of Satan, compiled a list of 82 adversarial or anti-hero figures from Sumerian, Babylonian, Greek, Roman, Hebrew, Hindu, Chinese, Japanese, Aztec, Mayan, Native American and African mythologies, intended for use in Satanic ritual. The list only represents what LeVey found to be the names most effectively used in Satanic ritual.

He published his 78 Infernal Names in his Satanic Bible, plus four Crown Princes of Hell, although there are only 81 names as Leviathan is listed twice. The four Crown Princes of Hell he sets apart as being particularly powerful are Satan, Lucifer, Beelzebub and Leviathan. Each prince is associated with a cardinal point of the compass and an element, as is common in western occultism.

All the Infernal Names are said to reside in the Royal Palace of Hell.

Goetic Spirits

Goetic spirits are those demons summoned by King Solomon who contained them in a bronze vessel and commanded to build his temple. In the modern mind, goetic spirits are the evil spirits associated with black magic. Thought to be based on the Fallen Angels of the Book of Enoch, in Solomonic magic they are the demons numerically paired with the 72 Angels of the Shemhamphorash, who protect the conjuror and control the demons he summons.

They take their name from the Ars Goetia or Howling Arts, the first section of the 17th century grimoire called the Lesser Keys of Solomon. Originally called the Spirits of the Seals, they are also known as the 72 Princes of the Hierarchy of Hell, the Spirits of the Brazen Vessel and the False Monarchy of Demons.

Goetic sigils were a subject of much interest to European magicians and the Christian Church. Those spirits identified as being amongst the 72 were re-classified as demons by the Christian church and became the subject of various grimoires like the Lesser Keys. Many devotees were shocked and dismayed at their spirits re-classification as a demon, in particularly those of Astaroth, previously the Goddess Astarte, before the church reassigned her name and gender. Described as commanded by the four kings of the cardinal directions, the goetic spirits are divided into two groups for white or black magic purposes. Combined, the spirits accomplish all abominations. While some of these spirits seem a little evil at first glance, practice shows that many of them perform useful tasks, such as healing and teach a great number of useful things, such as language and sciences. They are easy to command and are far from demonic in nature.

The Lesser Keys of Solomon differs from other goetic texts because entities are compelled into obedience, rather than asked for favours. In the 20th century, the Hermetic Order of the Golden Dawn revived Solomonic magic. The Ars Goetia portion of the Lesser Keys of Solomon was translated by S L Mathers and published by Aleister Crowley in 1904 under the title of The Book of the Goetia of Solomon the King.

3 Great Dukes of Hell
The sigils or seals of the three Great Dukes of Hell are first documented in the 1567 century grimoire titled Grimorium Verum or the Grimoire of Truth. They are Emperor Lucifer, Prince Beelzebub and Grand Duke Astaroth as the evil three, the Chief Demons of Hell.

The Sigil of Lucifer or the Sigillum Diabolus was first documented in the Verum Atca, the Grimoire of Truth, published in 1517. Its purpose was to be an instrument of visual invocation during ritual, acting as a gateway. By performing the appropriate ritual, to invoke and bestow the power and presence of Lucifer, Beelzebub or Astaroth. In modern times it has been adopted by Satanic and Luciferian cults as an emblem.

Its graphic appearance is a chalice which represents creation, the fertile darkness awaiting and ready for untold possibilities. As a sigil of Lucifer, as he is the bearer of light and wisdom into the darkness (that has been invoked by this sigil). The X over the chalice indicates the power and realm of the physical plane, as it iis passion and sensuality that drives all entities. The inverted triangle represents Water, often referred to as the 'original elixir of life' without which physical life could not exist. The 'V' at the bottom of the sigil represents the duality of all things, dark and light, male and female, etc., and as the power of convergence of the two into one manifesting balance, creation and existence.

Beelzebub is cited as a derogatory Jewish name for the Phoenician God Baal, husband of Astarte, Beelzebub is the name of a deity worshipped on the Philistine city of Ekron, originally thought to have meant Lord of the High Place (Heaven). The name we have now is probably a Hebrew variation designed to denigrate the deity as Lord of the Flies. In Christian texts, the name was that of a demon or devil. Jesus was accused of being an agent of Beelzebub, Lord of Flies, Prince of Demons.

In the 16th century, he was named as one of the three Chief Demons of Hell, an unholy trinity with Lucifer and Astaroth and was associated with witchcraft. In the 17th century, Milton names him as 'next to Satan' being second in rank of the Fallen Angels. In the 20th century, G.I. Gurdjieff and William Golden have used his name and character to discuss metaphysics and the reality of evil in man. In the 21st century, Australian occultist Barry William Hale published a grimoire of demonic magic for Beelzebub and his 49 servitors.

In Renaissance demonology, Astaroth is a male demon, one of the Great Dukes of Hell and one of the 72 goetic demons of Solomonic magic. Astaroth rules over various traits such as laziness, self-doubt and rationality. He also became associated with mathematics, which some scholars attributed to the religious backlash against the growing influence of science at the time. In cabala, he is an arch demon associated with the adverse force of the Qlipholth. In the Grimoirium Verum, he is the infernal principality which rules the America's.

His name, Astaroth, is thought to be derived from the Greek name for the Phoenician Goddess Astarte (Ishtar/Inanna), the wife of Baal. In the Bible she is referred to as Astoreth and considered as a false goddess of Yahweh. Despite her popularity, Astarte continued to be villainized throughout early Christianity and was understood to be a representation of pagan beliefs that should be rejected. By the Middle Ages, Astarte, like Baal was associated with the Christian Devil and was transformed in medieval works into the male demon Astaroth.

Luciferianism and Satanism

According to the Christian church, Devil worship has always existed and is a continual threat to the Kingdom of God's Heaven. Prior to the 20th century, Luciferianism was a form of medieval neo-Gnosticism and Satanism didn't exist. Both Luciferian and Satanic cults were born out of the religious persecutions that began in Europe in 1022 and lasted until the 18th century with the repeal of the anti-witchcraft laws. Both cults have their roots in the antithesis or anti-hero of the Christian God.

Luciferianisn began in the 13th or 14th century, attributed to a woman called Lucardis who wanted to restore Lucifer to his righteous place in heaven. For medieval neo-gnostic sects like the Bogomills, Cathars and Luciferians, Lucifer is the true God and the Old Testament God is the Demiurge, the Devil, the one responsible for imprisoning mankind in the material world.

Satan on the other hand is a modern construct based on religious, historical, artistic and philosophical interpretations of the central figure of evil in Christianity. This tradition began in the 14th century and remained underground until a resurgence in the 19th century, after which modern personalities such as Crowley, Sloane and LeVey developed its philosophies and initiated its Bible, Church and Temple. In the 21st century, a myriad of new sects exist in Europe, America and Australasia with widely different philosophies on the nature of their chosen deity.

The Crux Satana translates as Satan's Cross and is also known as Leviathan Cross. This elaborate symbol features two bars on the upright cross, symbolizing double protection and a balance between male and female. At the bottom of the cross is the infinity sign which also becomes the double Ouroborus. The cross also carries phallic connotations.

In alchemy, the Leviathan Cross is the symbol for Sulphur, one of the three essential elements of Nature, along with Salt and Mercury. The cross was originally used by both the Knights Templar and the Cathars, but there is no record of this particular cross having any connections to Satanism, prior to its adoption by Anton LeVey as a symbol for his Church of Satan.

Sigil of Baphomet

Originally a deity of the classical Levant – Palestine, Lebanon, Israel, Jordan, knowledge of Baphomet was brought back to Europe by the Templars, who were then persecuted by the Christian church for their supposed worship of him. The English word Baphomet comes from the medieval Latin Baphometh. It is now thought that the Templars were Gnostics and the word comes from the Greek term Baphe Metous or Baptism of Wisdom. When translated into Hebrew and cabalistically interpreted using the Atbash cipher and reversed, it translates as Sophia or Wisdom.

Baphomet is most famous as the Sabbatic Goat, Eliphas Levi's image of a man sat cross legged with the head, legs and feet of a goat with a pentagram on its forehead and a pair of wings. Aleister Crowley used Levi's image as his source for the Devil in his Tarot pack and took the name Baphomet as his motto.

The Sigil of Baphomet was a 19th century French design called the Goat of Mendes, comprised of the head of a goat transfixed upon a reversed pentagram flanked by Hebrew letters of the word 'Leviathan'. It was adopted as the official emblem of the Church of Satan by Anton LeVey in the 1960s. Another version shows the names Samuel and Lilith in the center circle.

Lilith

There are fewer female demons than male and they are mostly associated with infant mortality, infidelity and disobedience. Their roles and influence having been expanded over time from biblical and cabalistic sources. Originating in the Middle East, they passed through Sumerian, Akkadian, Babylonian, Phoenician, Hebrew and Christian lore into Medieval and Renaissance demonology, as exemplified by Astarte's rebranding as the male demon Astaroth. Female deities from Greco-Egyptian sources such as Isis and Hekate are more associated with witchcraft than being described as demons.

The oldest known female demon is the Sumerian deity called Tiamat, wife of the principle being Apsu. The Supreme God Marduk engaged her in battle, resulting in an epic struggle and after finally defeating her, he created the world from her corpse. This story is told in the Babylonian creation epic called the 'Enuma Elish'. Both Tiamat and Marduk are invoked in the 'Simon' Necronomicon.

The main female demon in western occultism is Lilith. Originally a Sumerian demon who made her way into Jewish lore, she is the archetypical female demon of Judeo-Christian theology. Lilith is mentioned only once in passing in the Bible, but she is fleshed out in later sources, particularly in folk tradition. A 10th century source, 'The Alphabet of Ben Shira' tells us that Lilith was the first wife of Adam who insisted on equality between them and refused to return to him. Her refusal to lie beneath Adam set the archetypical example for later feminists and pagan feminists.

Medieval legends said that all witches are descended from the biblical Lilith. Lilith's myth goes on to say that she mated with demons and in doing so became one herself, a demonic source of child deaths. Her children with other demons became the Illim or Succibi, who wander the world seducing men to mate with them, and birth more succibi in the process. The Incubus or Incubi are the male equivalent of the Succabus or Succibi.

Agrat bat Mahlet meaning 'Daughter of Mahlet' is a demoness from Jewish mythology. Rabbinic literature identifies her as the daughter of the demon Lilith. It also identifies her as a demon who haunts the skies riding a chariot accompanied by 18 other demons. It also mentions her as one of the many demons who taught forbidden magic to humanity. Cabala identifies her as a Fallen Angel and one of the consorts of the Fallen Angel Samael. It also associates her with sacred prostitution, a practice associated with the Babylonian Goddess Ishtar/Astarte.

Naamah is another demoness from Jewish literature. She first appeared in the Zohar, the first book of the cabalistic tradition. The Zohar describes her as a Fallen Angel who repeatedly seduces Adam to have demonic children with him. She also worked with Lilith to seduce the angles Azazel and Ousa, causing them to fall from grace.

But her roots are in the Talmudic-Midrashic tradition which describes her as the sister of Tubal-Cain, one of the people who lived before the Great Flood. She had a reputation as seductress and even managed to seduce the Fallen Angel Shamdon and became pregnant with the demonic Prince Ashmodai.

The Abominations of the Necronomicon

The post-modern grimore the 'Simon' Necronomicon contains the names and sigils of many Sumerian derived demons with unpronounceable names with frightening meanings. The sigils of the Abominations are from The Urilia Text or Book of Worms, which contains the formula by which the wreakers of havoc perfom their rites.

The Abominations are the terrible offspring of the Ancient Ones that may be summoned by the priest. They were begotten before all ages and dwelt in the blood of Kingu. They dwell beyond the Gate of the Outside and may be summoned when Marduk is not worshipped and sleeps on those days when he has no power.

Chief among the Ancient Ones is Cthulhu, a water element typified as a sea monster, dwelling in the Great Deep, a sort of primeval ocean. Cthulhu is an interpretation of the Sumerian name Kutulu meaning The Man of the Underworld or Satan. Kutulu (Cthulhu) is the Sleeping Lord. He is accompanied by an assortment of other grotesques such as Shub Niggurath

Of All the Gods and All the Spirits of Abomination, there cane be no use or gain to call upon Azag – Thoth, as he is surely mad. Rendered sightless in the Battle, He is Lord of Chaos and the priest can find little use for him. Thus, for that reason, his seal is not given.

The Dark Angel Humwawa is The Lord of the Abominations. Pazuzu is the grinning Dark Angel of the Four Wings and Lord of All Fevers and Plagues. Azag-Thoth is the blind, mad, Lord of Chaos.

Other demons include, Akhkharu who sucketh the blood from man. Lalassu who haunteth the places of man. Lalartu who is caught between worlds. Lamashta the Queen of Sickness and Misery. Xaster the foul demoness who slays men in their sleep and devours that which she will. The Scorpion Man who dwells in the mountains of old, who was created by Tiamat to fight the Elder Gods. And the Incubus called Gelial, who invades the beds of women and the Succibus called Lilit who invades the beds of men. These are the legions of the Evil Ones.

Legion 49

Legion 49 is a post-modern grimoire published by Fulgar Press in 2007. It is a title is taken from the 49 servitors of the Archdemon Beelzebub created by Australian artist and occultist Barry William Hale. In Legion 49, Hale explores traditional and modern methods of evocation by providing a creatively innovative, iconographical and sigillic recension of Beelzebub and his servitors.

Hale has used a lifetime of knowledge on the summoning of Beelzebub and his 49 servants or servitors, taking their names and powers from the chthonic pantheon of the Mexican Amerindian paper cut tradition of 'Papal Picardo' a folk craft associated with the Day of the Dead altars, which he fused with Spanish Inquisition demonology to the servitors of Beelzebub found in the Renaissance grimoire the Sacred Magic of Abramelin, as interpreted by the Golden Dawn. This, he combined with a list of psychically received images of the servitors, enough to produce the creatively innovative shadow-cut figures that act as sigils for Beelzebub and his servitor's.

DEMONIC SPIRITS

ABYSS
Lord of Chaos

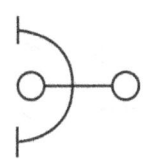

ACIEL
The God Burner

ADATIEL
Walks the Earth

ADNACHIEL
The Hunter Demon

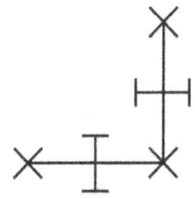

AGIEL
Lord of Calamity

AMBRIEL
The Chancer

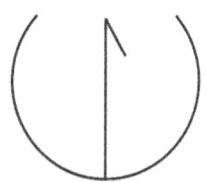

AMNIXIEL
Demon of the Lines

ANAEL
Demon of Lust

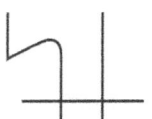

APADIEL
Od Hell's Electorate
"MUSICIAN"

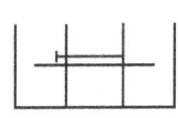

ARATRON
Demon of Sorrow

ARIEL
Of Hell's Electoraye
"HISTORIAN"

AVACHIEL
The Noursitor

Agrippa's Demons

SIGILS, SEALS AND PENTACLES

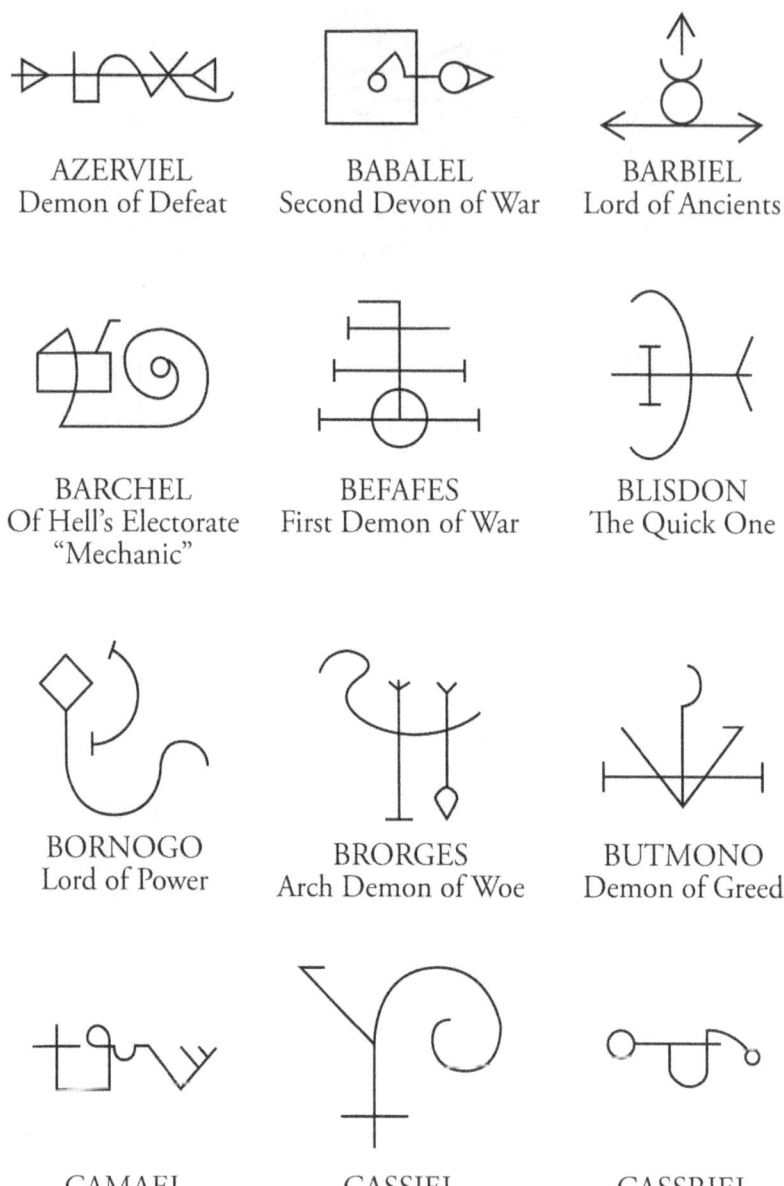

AZERVIEL
Demon of Defeat

BABALEL
Second Devon of War

BARBIEL
Lord of Ancients

BARCHEL
Of Hell's Electorate
"Mechanic"

BEFAFES
First Demon of War

BLISDON
The Quick One

BORNOGO
Lord of Power

BRORGES
Arch Demon of Woe

BUTMONO
Demon of Greed

CAMAEL
The Destroyer

CASSIEL
Lord of All
Conspirators

CASSRIEL
Of Hell's Electorate
"POET"

Agrippa's Demons

DEMONIC SPIRITS

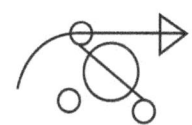

EOLIGOS
Visable and Invisable

FERUG
The Rusting One

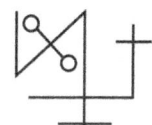

FOCALOR
The Demon That Drowns Men

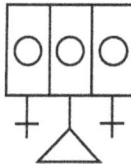

FORCAS
Teaches Logics and the Secrets of Plants and Gems

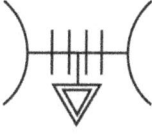

FURTUR
Demon of Storms

GAMIGIN
The Horse Lord

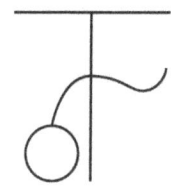

GARN
The King Tempter

GRACHIEL
Arch Demon of the Dying Times

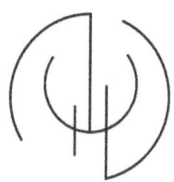

HAGITH
Demon of Jealousy

HAGONEL
Lord Under Grachiel

HAMALIEL
Lord of Obsessions

HANAEL
The Adversarial

Agrippa's Demons

HASMODEL &
HASMODAI
The Twin Bulls

HISMAEL
The Acouirer

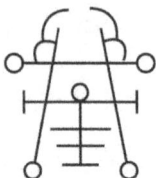

IPOS
Knows Things
To Come and Past

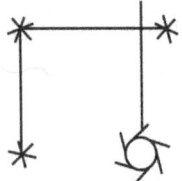

JOCHMUS
The First Savior
of Hell

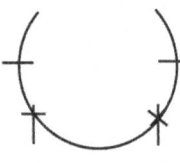

LAHAD
The Devil Voice

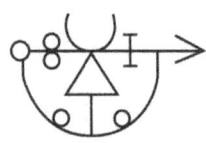

LESIFUGES
Brings Riches and
Shortens Life

LUCIFER
The Morning Star

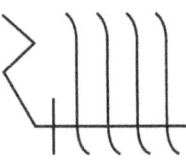

MALCHIDAEL
Demon of Impatience

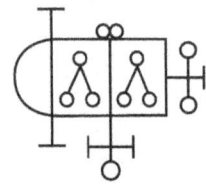

MALPHAS
The Tower Builder

MARBUEL
Of Hell's Electorate
"ARCHITECT"

MARCHOSIAS
Gives Aid in Battle
A Demon Bound

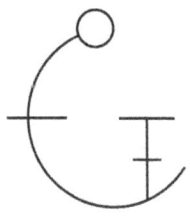

MEEOD
The Life Restorer

Agrippa's Demons

DEMONIC SPIRITS

MEPHISTOPH
Lord of the Host

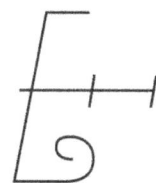

MICZARIEL
The Warrioress

MURIEL
Great Demon of Lies

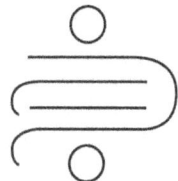

NABERIUS
Lord of Cunning

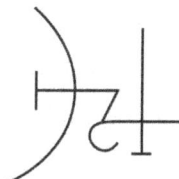

NESTORATS
The Fire Master

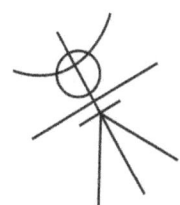

NYSROG
Lord of the House
of Princes

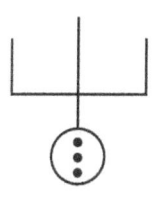

OCH
The Sun Speaker

OPHIEL
Lord Messenger and
God Teacher

ORIAS
Of Hell's Electorate
"ASTRONOMER"

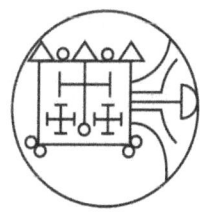

OZGIN
Demon of Madness

PAIMON
Master of Infernal
Ceremonies

Agrippa's Demons

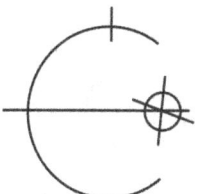

PARNIEL
First Lord Under
VECUANIEL

SIGILS, SEALS AND PENTACLES

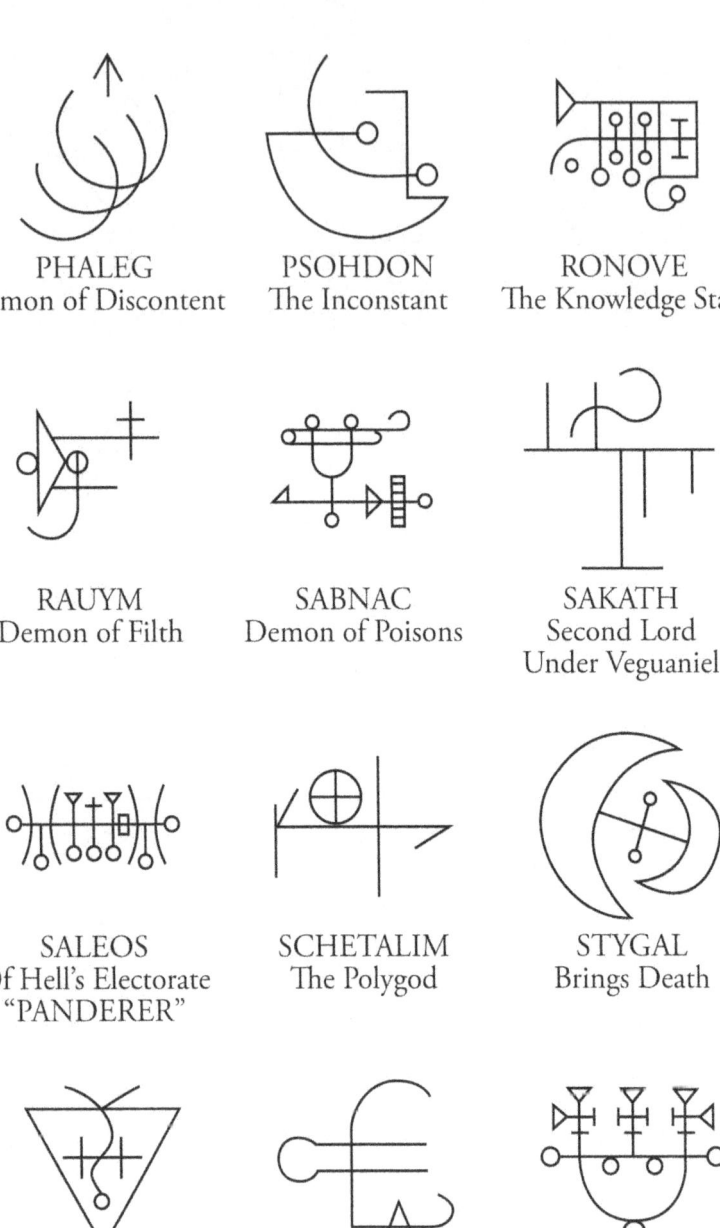

| PHALEG
Demon of Discontent | PSOHDON
The Inconstant | RONOVE
The Knowledge Staff |

| RAUYM
Demon of Filth | SABNAC
Demon of Poisons | SAKATH
Second Lord
Under Veguaniel |

| SALEOS
Of Hell's Electorate
"PANDERER" | SCHETALIM
The Polygod | STYGAL
Brings Death |

| SULUTH
The Great Robber | SURGAT
Who Opens All Locks | SYTRI
Lord of Luxury |

Agrippa's Demons

DEMONIC SPIRITS

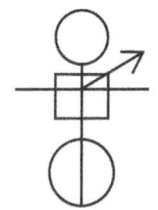

TARTHANAC
Lord of Coldiron

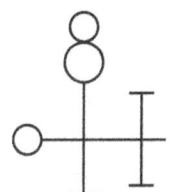

TEPHROS
The Ashmaker and
Fever Curer

UPHIR
Of Hell's Electorate
"PHYSKIAN"

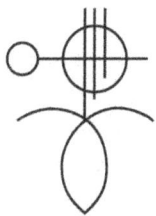

VABAM
Who Tells True of
Hidden Treasures

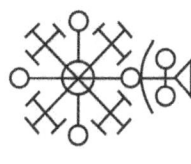

VALAC
Lord of Snakes

VEGUANIEL
Arch Demon
of Fortune

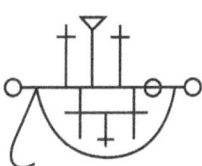

VEPAR
The Water Master

VETIS
The Life Promser

ZABALH
OF Hell's Electorate
"LAWYER"

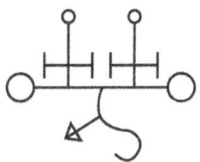

ZAGAM
Lord of Forgery

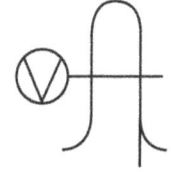

ZURIEL
The Stone Master

ZEPAR
Deforms the Unborn

Agrippa's Demons

Seals of the Spirits - Lesser Key of Solomon - Ars Goetia

DEMONIC SPIRITS

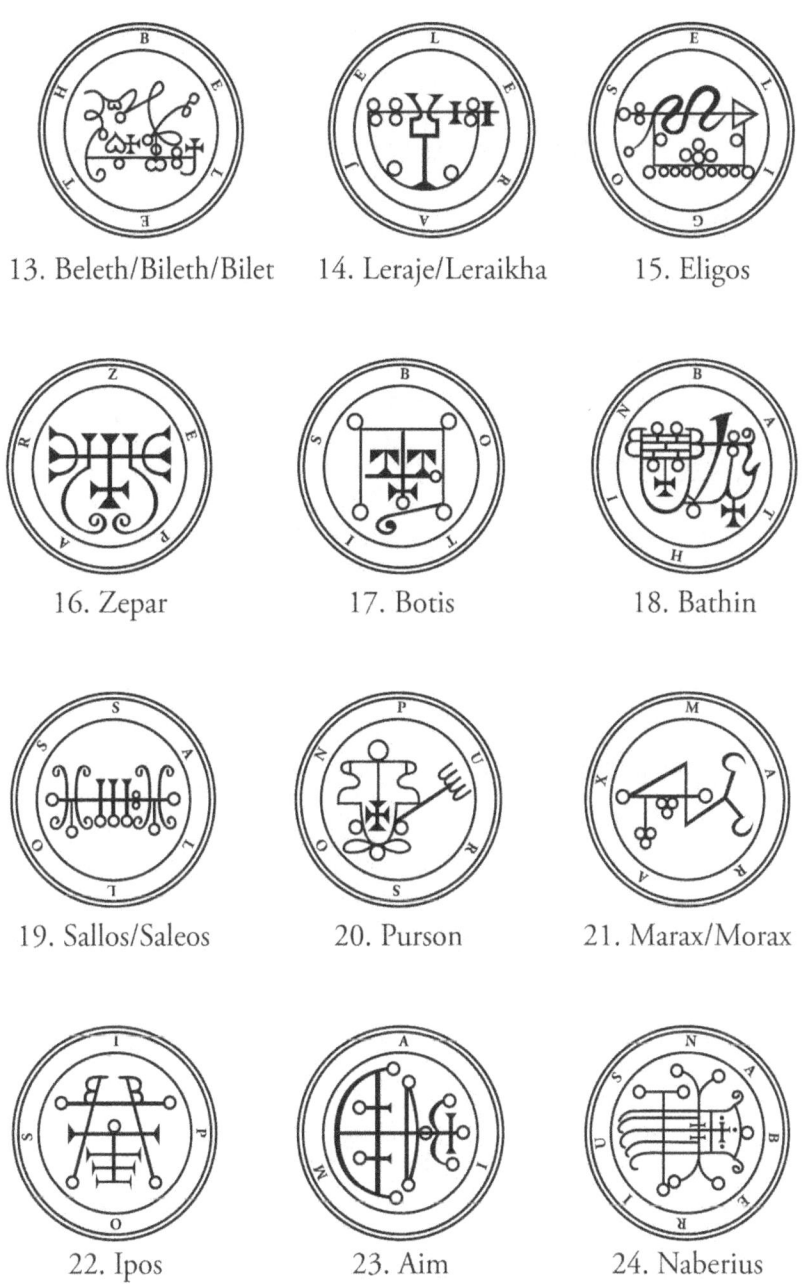

13. Beleth/Bileth/Bilet   14. Leraje/Leraikha   15. Eligos

16. Zepar   17. Botis   18. Bathin

19. Sallos/Saleos   20. Purson   21. Marax/Morax

22. Ipos   23. Aim   24. Naberius

Seals of the Spirits - Lesser Key of Solomon - Ars Goetia

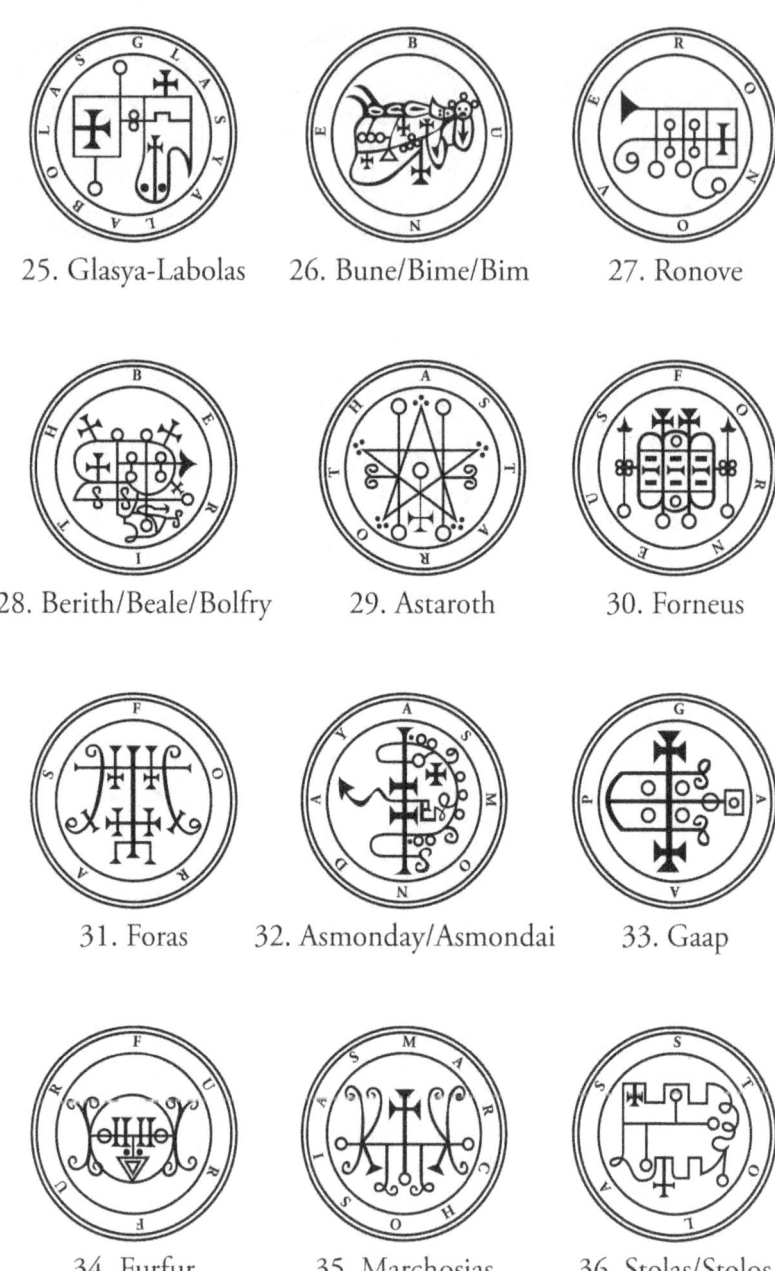

Seals of the Spirits - Lesser Key of Solomon - Ars Goetia

DEMONIC SPIRITS

37. Phenex/Pheynix   38. Halphas   39. Malphas/Malthus

40. Raum   41. Focalor/Forcalor   42. Vepar/Vephar

43. Sabnock   44. Shan/Shax/Shaz/Shass   45. Vine/Vinea

46. Bifrons/Bifrous   47. Uvall/Vual   48. Haagenti

Seals of the Spirits - Lesser Key of Solomon - Ars Goetia

Seals of the Spirits - Lesser Key of Solomon - Ars Goetia

DEMONIC SPIRITS

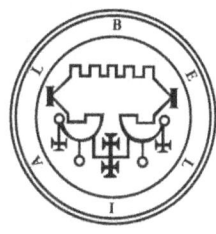

61. Zagan   62. Volac/Valu/Ualac/Valac   63. Andras

64. Haures/Flauros   65. Andrealphus   66. Cimejes/Kimaris

67. Amdusias/Amdukias   68. Belial   69. Decarabia

70. Seere/Sear/Seir   71. Dantalion   72. Andromalius

Seals of the Spirits - Lesser Key of Solomon - Ars Goetia

SIGILS, SEALS AND PENTACLES

Sigillum Diabolus

Full Sigil of Lucifer

Sigil of Beelzebub

Sigil of Astaroth

The Great Dukes of Hell - Grimoirium Verum

SIGILS, SEALS AND PENTACLES

Sulphur / Brimstone - Lucifer and Satan

Phosphorous - Lucifer
(Morning Star)

Antimony - Satan
(Grey Wolf)

Crux Satana / Leviathan Cross

Satan's Cross Reversed

Sulpher / Brimstone - Satan and Leviathann

Alchemical Symbols for Lucifer, Satan and Leviathann

DEMONIC SPIRITS 193

Reverse Cross

Question Mark Cross

Satanic Cross

The Satanic Temple

Six Six Six
Number of the Beast

Satanic Pentagram and
Reverse Ctoss

Satanic Symbols

SIGILS, SEALS AND PENTACLES

Goat of Mendes / Sigil of Baphomet

Seal   Great Seal

Seals of the Demoness Lilith

DEMONIC SPIRITS

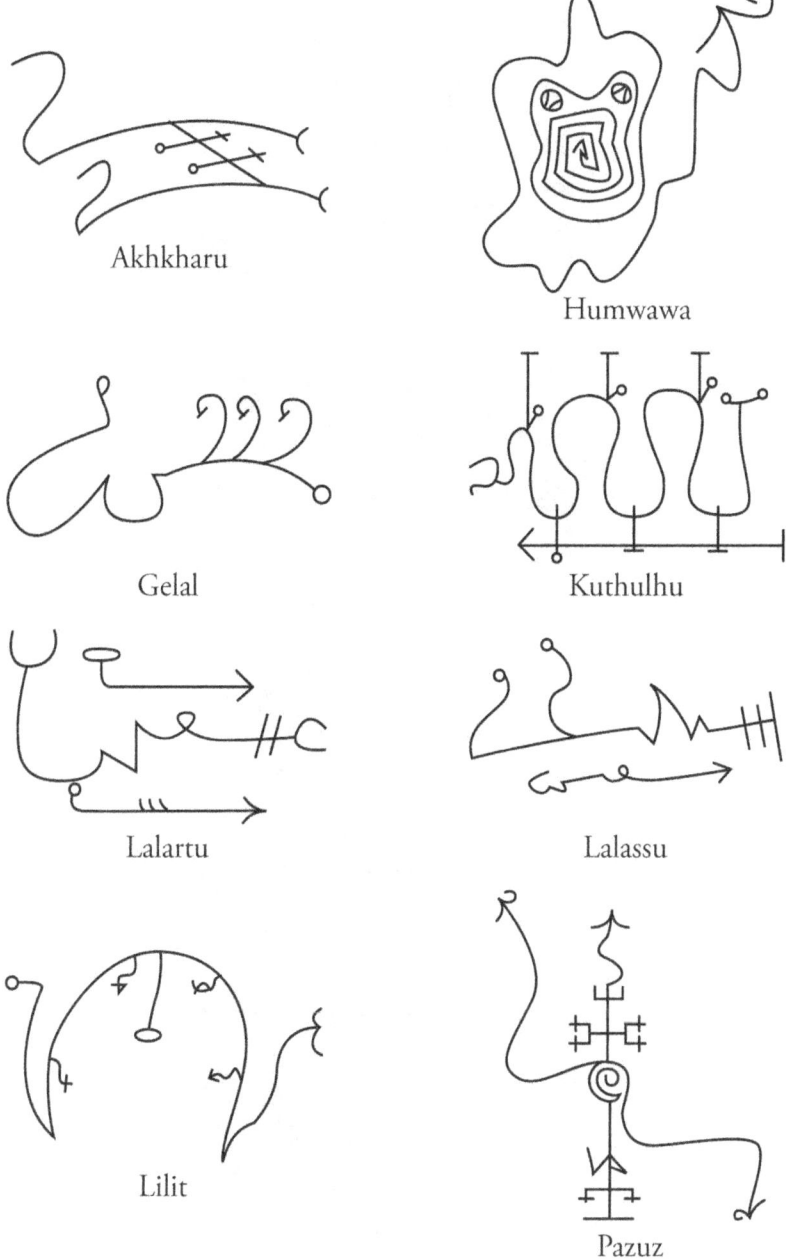

Sigils of the Abominations - 'Simon' Necronomicon

Shadow-Cut Sigils
Legion 49 - William Barry Hale

DEMONIC SPIRITS

Shadow-Cut Sigils
Legion 49 - William Barry Hale

Shadow-Cut Sigil for Beelzebub
Legion 49 - William Barry Hale

Further Reading

PRINT

Sefer Raziel – Hebrew
6th & 7th Books of Moses – Hebrew
Picatrix (Ghayat al Hakim) – Arabic
Book of Honorus – Honorus of Thebes
Livres de Espiritz – anonymous
Grimorium Verum anonymous
Biblioteca Magn Rabbinica – Bartolozi
Verum Arca – anonymous
Heptameron – anonymous
Sacred Magic of Abramelin – anonymous
Polygraphia – Johannes Trithemius
Da Occulta Philosophie – Heirich Cornelius Agrippa
Psuedomonarchia Deamonum – Johannes Weyer
Aratabel of Magic – anonymous
The Flock of Abraham – Abraham De Bolines
Magical Treatise of Solomon – anonymous
Key of Solomon – anonymous
Lesser Key of Solomon – anonymous
Mystica Hepatachia – Dr. John Dee
Black Venus – Dr. John Dee
Liber Loagaeth – Dr. John Dee
Book of Aramadel – anonymous
Black Pullet – anonymous
The Magus – Francis Barrett
La Clef de la Magie – Stanislav de Guaire

PRINT (continued)

History of Magic – Eliphas Levi
The Book od Goetia of Solomon the King – S L Mathers
Holy Book of Thelema – Aleister Crowley
Book of Pleasure – Austin Osman Spare
Book of Shadows – Gerald Gardner
Satanic Bible – Anton LeVey
Master Grimoire of Magical Rites and Ceremonies – Nathan Elkman
Necronomicon – Simon
Al Azif – Book of Dead Names – Wilson Hay Turner Langford
Al Azif – The Necronomicon – Dr. John Dee
13 Gates of the Necronomicon – Donald Tyson
Legion 49 – Barry William Hale

WEB
sacredtexts.com
esotericarchive.com
occult-study.org
wordpress.com
archive.com
lwelyn.com
encyclopedia.com
wikipedia.com

www.ingramcontent.com/pod-product-compliance
Lightning Source LLC
Chambersburg PA
CBHW061305110426
42742CB00012BA/2068